MORE MEMORIES
OF
ROCHDALE

TRUE NORTH BOOKS

DEAN CLOUGH

HALIFAX

WEST YORKSHIRE

HX3 5AX

TEL 01422 344344

THE PUBLISHERS WOULD LIKE TO THANK THE
FOLLOWING COMPANIES FOR SUPPORTING THE
PRODUCTION OF THIS BOOK

AFTER EIGHT RESTAURANT

BIWATER TREATMENT LIMITED

HARTLEY, THOMAS & WRIGHT

HOPWOOD HALL COLLEGE

LANE BOTTOM IEP SOCIETY LIMITED

LEACH & CLEGG JOINERY

MABYRN RUBBER COMPANY LIMITED

ROCHDALE EXCHANGE SHOPPING CENTRE

ROCHDALE TRAINING ASSOCIATION LIMITED

UNITED SPRINGS LIMITED

VENTURE PRECISION ENGINEERING LIMITED

WEST PENNINE INSURANCE GROUP

WHEATSHEAF SHOPPING CENTRE

VA WHITLEY & COMPANY LIMITED

First published in Great Britain by True North Books
Dean Clough
Halifax HX3 5AX
1998

ISBN 1 900 463 22 9

Introduction

The publication of our first book, *Memories of Rochdale,* met with a tremendous response from the people in the town. Thousands of copies of the original book have been sold to date, with many finding their way overseas to bring pleasure to former Rochdale residents who had emigrated. The letters of encouragement and kind comments we received urged us to produce a second book, this time containing even more of the excellent photographs which had provided such enjoyment. The compilation of *More Memories of Rochdale* has been carried out over a period of several months. We always expected it to be a pleasurable experience, but in the event the satisfaction we have derived from studying the marvellous old photographs went far beyond our expectations.

Smith Street in the 1950s

Increasingly, nostalgia is enjoyed by a growing band of people and the book is intended to appeal to a wide audience. Where possible we have tried to concentrate upon a period within the memory of most of our readers; the 1950s, 60s and 70s - decades which saw tremendous changes in the town, and a time when changes in the world of work, entertainment, public health and retailing continued to thrive. Change takes place constantly in every town and Rochdale is no exception. As we all get older it is often easier to 'step back' and view events and developments with a clearer sense of perspective. Our aim has been to assist in this respect by presenting a 'catalyst' capable of rekindling memories of days gone by in an entertaining manner.

Looking through the pages of this book it may be surprising how much change has taken place, and over such a relatively short period, relative to the long history of the area. Several of Rochdale's best known and longest established firms have allowed us access to their often extensive internal archives. This has enabled us to recount the history of these companies, from humble beginnings to, in most cases, leading positions in their chosen area of expertise. Of course, these organisations have tremendous social, as well as commercial significance, as between them they represent the places of employment for thousand upon thousand Rochdale people. We are grateful for the co-operation and support of the directors of these businesses for adding to the quality and interest of this book.

Many of the children featured in these photographs will be reaching retirement age now and we would be pleased to hear from anyone who may have recognised themselves.

Street scenes are not neglected. Photographs of this nature were popular in the last book, and understandably so. The changing face of the town is reflected in the way our roads and shops have developed to meet the changing needs of our lives over the years. These photographs show the shops and motorcars we remember from our early days, along with the fashions which were all the rage when we were younger. All combine to refresh our memories of days gone by, and when that occurs the book will have achieved its aim.

We hope that you enjoy reading *More Memories of Rochdale* as much as we enjoyed creating it.

CAPTION RESEARCH AND COMPILATION...KEVIN MCILROY

DESIGNERS...................MANDY WALKER, NICKY BRIGHTON AND CHRISTINE GALE

COPYWRITER..PAULINE BELL

BUSINESS DEVELOPMENT EDITOR..ALAN EASTHAM

CONTENTS

SECTION ONE

EVENTS AND OCCASIONS

•

SECTION TWO

AROUND THE TOWN CENTRE

•

SECTION THREE

FLASH, BANG, WALLOP - WHAT A PICTURE!

•

SECTION FOUR

ON THE MOVE

•

SECTION FIVE

WHAT A PARADE

•

SECTION SIX

SHOPPING SPREE

•

SECTION SEVEN

AT WORK

Events and occasions

Like every town, village or city in this country Rochdale was expected to make vigorous efforts to financially contribute to the cost of fighting the 1914 to 1918 First World War and the 'war to end all wars' was, as it transpired later, incorrectly labelled. The good causes, often instigating from the Mayor's office, included, as we see here, buying a tank. These appeals were generally accompanied by a plea to give so that 'Rochdale would be spared the horrors of invasion by German troops'. Efforts were made throughout the town and surrounding villages and communities to contribute to the Army Christmas Pudding Fund, the Soldiers' Tobacco Fund, the Mayoress' Comfort Fund and there was one dedicated to Serbian

Relief. There were many others as the public was urged to give funds to maintain local regiments. These at the beginning of the war had sought to rely on volunteers' patriotic sense of duty after the call from Lord Kitchener that their country needed them. And they were told it would be all over by the first Christmas. However, that was not to be and, as the war dragged on and on, conscription was introduced. Conscription Boards were established in every town and acted like a magistrate's court and would summon to them men who had to explain why they had not joined up. The excuse that he did not know there was a war on, made by a farmer from the hills outside Rochdale, cut very little ice with the Board.

Spectators gather in Packer Street and also above on the grassy slopes of Broadfield Park to watch the crowds of Whit Walk marchers gather under the protective shadow of Rochdale's parish church for the traditional service after the procession around the town. Each local church and Sunday School walked, led by a banner announcing who they were and where they came from. This Whit or Pentecost Sunday was part of the then national Bank Holiday weekend and the town was thronged with visitors who came to watch and maybe join in with the service. It is very difficult to imagine what role the policemen have in this because order and attention are so evident as the crowd face the clergy in St Chad's gardens for hymns and prayers and a blessing. The Sunday School children also had a treat on the Friday when they all assembled on the Whit Friday Field, as they named it, for tea and games and this would surely have been a much looked forward-to event as part of the whole festival. This photograph gives an excellent idea of how the church and the vicarage command a view over the then heart of the town. That has been the case since the 12th century when a church was built here on the site of a Saxon Church and it was appropriate that in 1964, to celebrate 800 years of recorded history, the church should be honoured by a visit from Her Majesty the Queen and the Duke of Edinburgh.

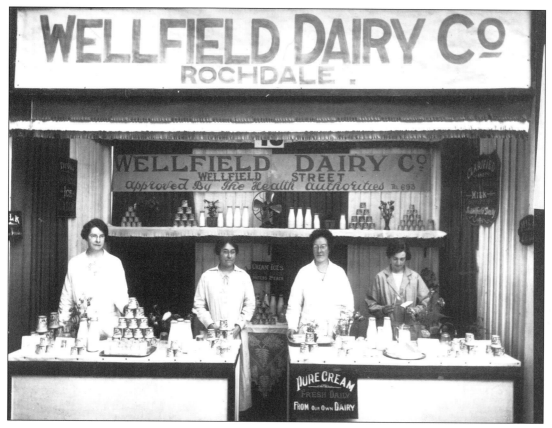

Above: The important sign here in a town with a very health conscious Public Health Department states that the milk from Wellfield Dairy is 'approved'. The dairy's stall shown here was in the Drill Hall in the 1930s but the dairy itself was part of the Wellfield Estate owned since 1830 by the Royds family and this enterprise was run by Mr J R Williams and his family. What is left of the estate is the old hall, now divided into two houses, situated between Oldham Road and the Kwik Save complex on Well i' th' Lane. It is very difficult to imagine that there stood houses, barns, meadows, corn mills, cotton mills, soapworks and a very thriving stone pop bottle enterprise, also under the guiding hand of Mr Williams who could boast that he supplied these unique bottles to such famous names as Bass, Guinness and Wheatley's Hot Bitters. He could also promise that he could supply at a very short notice lemonade, soda and ginger ale to schools and clubs and other such organisations. This family element is very strong as it is believed that of the four ladies in the photograph three are sisters, members of the Williams family. The dairy lasted until the 1950s when no doubt it was forced to close as people's shopping habits changed and big business took over seeing to all our needs.

Right: This historic photograph taken on 9th May 1910 shows the Mayor of Rochdale, Councillor George Dinning, announcing the death the previous day of King Edward VII and the accession to the throne of George V. The Mayor had received these sad tidings at 7.15 that morning. By means of the telephone, the use of an advertising cart, the police delivering handbills and a personal visit by the mayor to the Police Court, the populace was summoned to the Town Hall at 1pm. Mills, workshops and schools closed and a large crowd 'as far as the eye could see' gathered on The Esplanade. At 1 pm a trumpet call heralded the Mayor who then read the Royal Proclamation. The news was received in silence as the Mayor had wished until a Councillor Howarth, asked for three cheers for the new King. This was 'received quite heartily.' Then Alderman Cunliffe asked for three cheers for the new Queen Mary and this was received 'more lustily.' Generally, however, sorrow was the mood of the day.

After this the Mayor's party adjourned to the Mayor's parlour and the health of the new King was 'cordially honoured.' On the 20th May, the day of the late King's funeral, a civic requiem service was held and later memorial services took place in various chapels and churches in the town. Rochdale had given due and appropriate recognition to the death of its monarch.

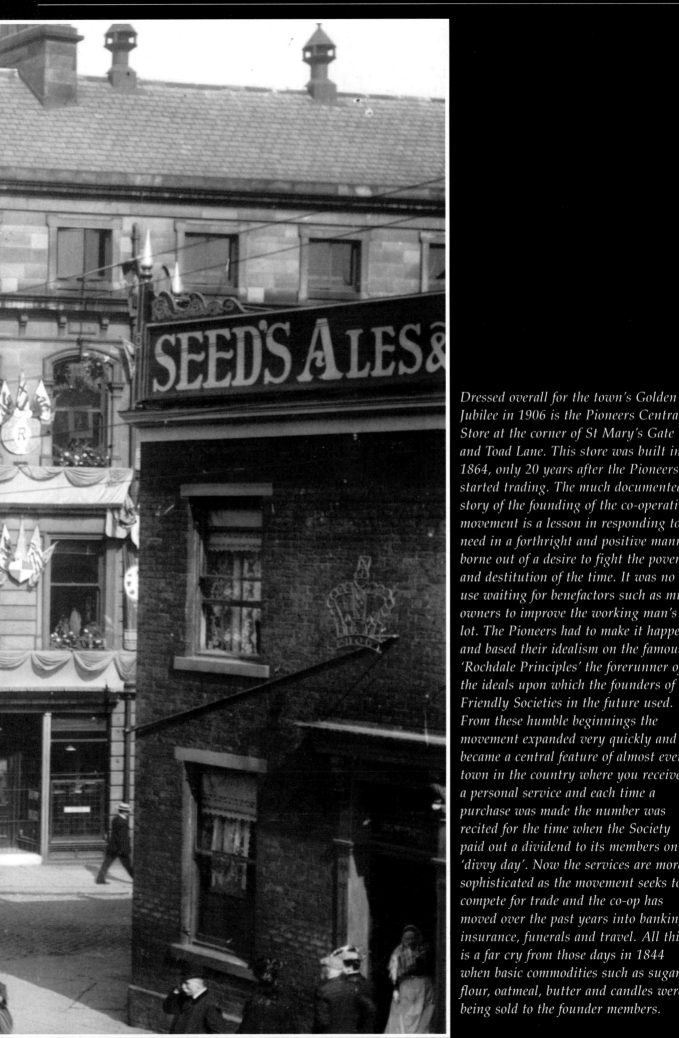

Dressed overall for the town's Golden Jubilee in 1906 is the Pioneers Central Store at the corner of St Mary's Gate and Toad Lane. This store was built in 1864, only 20 years after the Pioneers started trading. The much documented story of the founding of the co-operative movement is a lesson in responding to need in a forthright and positive manner borne out of a desire to fight the poverty and destitution of the time. It was no use waiting for benefactors such as mill-owners to improve the working man's lot. The Pioneers had to make it happen and based their idealism on the famous 'Rochdale Principles' the forerunner of the ideals upon which the founders of Friendly Societies in the future used. From these humble beginnings the movement expanded very quickly and became a central feature of almost every town in the country where you received a personal service and each time a purchase was made the number was recited for the time when the Society paid out a dividend to its members on 'divvy day'. Now the services are more sophisticated as the movement seeks to compete for trade and the co-op has moved over the past years into banking, insurance, funerals and travel. All this is a far cry from those days in 1844 when basic commodities such as sugar, flour, oatmeal, butter and candles were being sold to the founder members.

The town of Rochdale celebrated the Golden Jubilee of its incorporation as a municipal borough in September 1906 in great style. During the week long celebrations there were church services of thanksgiving and receptions, including a grand one for the borough's teachers, a banquet, which to describe it as magnificent would be an understatement (although the mayor was at pains to point out that the cost did not fall on the citizens of the town). The public highlight of the week took place in good weather on the final Saturday, September 9th, with a grand parade and civic procession. The preparation for this in terms of organisation, of dressing the floats and the control of the crowds was detailed and thorough. It took over one and a half hours for any one part of the procession to pass any given point on the five mile route around the decorated streets of the town. The whole procession eventually returned to its starting place, which was naturally the Town Hall. 18000 children were allotted the best roped off viewing points as they watched over 50 highly decorated floats thrill them and afterwards were entertained to tea in local schoolrooms. The vast crowds, employing every vantage point to gain a good view, were so enthralled by it all that, according to one report, the town's public houses were almost empty all afternoon. 'A triumph of good order' was one official verdict. Rochdalians and visitors who had poured into the town from Manchester and other northern towns marvelled at the spectacle. In fact, one visitor was heard to remark

that Manchester could not have bettered it. High praise indeed! The reception given to the military parade, especially the Yeomenry, was a great one and the laughter at the display of old fashioned fire fighting equipment from the 16th and 18th centuries was taken in good part by the local firemen who were very proud to show how well equipped the modern firemen of Rochdale were. Floats representing all aspects of work, business and leisure took part and they included the Rochdale Chrysanthemum Society's which was very intricate to say the least. It consisted of cart with a nine feet tall bamboo plant in the centre, with palms and Australian pines at each corner and in the centre masses of hydrangeas, geraniums, coleii and sweet peas. Rochdale Corporation's farm at Roch Mills had an agricultural tableaux, described as 'tastefully displayed', full of farm produce.

Other outstanding displays came from the town's public service departments like the Rochdale Transport float (bottom left). There were entries from the Handyman's Association, the Textile Trades, the Woollen Mutual Improvement Society and of Weaving and Carding and Spinning equipment throughout the years. There was a children's tableaux from Spotland Council School entitled 'Japanese Tea'. One display which sparked great interest was from the British Cotton Growers Association with bales of British cotton accompanied, according to a local newspaper report of the event, by 'darkies from Africa'. It was generally agreed, however, that the highlight of the procession was the Rushcart. This consisted of rushes gathered from Blackstone Edge being formed into a pyramid, the construction being put together in

Lowerplace with the help of an expert from Crompton. On the day itself the horse drawn cart was accompanied by 30 men from Lowerplace similarly attired in white shirts and stockings, light-blue breeches and dark-blue caps with on their feet decorated clogs. The Jubilee reached a splendid climax in the evening with a massive fireworks display on the park slopes behind the Town Hall where the most remarkable scenes were witnessed by a vast crowd. They were thrilled by whistling rockets, a monster balloon shedding coloured lights, a device outlining a Saxon Cross, another displaying the Maltese Star and a comic device which portrayed an acrobat walking a tightrope. These and many more too enchanted the crowd who had this day publicly demonstrated their pride in their town in a remarkable manner.

The novel idea of having your photograph taken seems to have appealed to the seated crowd outside the Denehurst house for the ceremonial presentation in July 1932 by Mr Samuel Turner J.P. to the Mayor, Councillor W. Crossley of the family residence and grounds to the town. The Mayor had opened the gates to Denehurst with a gold key and here the invited guests are to witness the handing over the deeds of the house. The acquisition of 'the beauty and amenity of the estate' was regarded quite understandably as a great event although at the time there was a public debate as to how to make use of the house with the easier decision that grounds were to be used as a public park. The ceremony concluded with the Mayoress planting a tree, followed by a display of drill, physical exercises and country dancing by local scholars with music provided by the Shawclough and Spotland Prize Band. Now Denehurst park could be added to the list of civic amenities like Broadfield Park which were donated to the town and which any industrial town like Rochdale required for the recreation of its citizens. Often it is very easy to forget the many assets industrial towns like Rochdale have on their doorstep including gardens and parks like Denehurst, museums, nature reserves and trails, lakes and sporting facilities and which have all been made available for the public good and which should only be ignored at our peril.

Hundreds of excited local folk can be seen posing for the camera in this photograph taken along the Esplanade. It certainly makes a breathtaking sight and it is impossible not to be impressed by all these folk waiting quietly for the photographer to take his picture. A clue to the reason for the celebrations can be found on the left of the photograph, in the hand of the smartly dressed Boy Scout. The hand bill reads "Official Souvenir Coronation Programme." Clearly the Coronation in question was either that of George VI (May 1937) or the 1953 event honouring our present Queen Elizabeth II. In dating the photograph we come up against a dilemma. It this was really a 1930s picture we would expect more of the lads to be wearing caps -especially for a photograph like this, and some of the clothes (such as those worn by the lady next to the St. John's Ambulance men) look decidedly '1950s.' And the medals worn by those ambulance men were won in either the First or Second World War - some 19 years before if this is 1937... or just seven years before if the picture relates to the last Coronation. The ladies on the right of the picture appear to be wearing clothing typical of the 1930s, but most of us will remember a time when our elderly relatives preferred the fashions of their youth and saw nothing wrong in sticking to them. 1930s or 1950s? - we'll leave the choice up to you.

It is very hard to realise that in the age in which we now live that we did not 'invent' concern for the environment, recycling and other 'green' causes. The problems which confront us today concerning the effects of domestic and industrial waste and other issues which affect peoples' health and standard of living or as it is termed today, quality of life, have for many, many years been faced by forward thinking public health bodies such as the one existing in Rochdale.

Public health issues in any industrial town had to be addressed and the story of how the borough's departments dealt with them must surely have acted as a model for other industrial towns. The growth in industry and business lead to an equally large growth in the need for the local council to pay a greater regard to the health of its citizens. This can be dated back to the late 1800s when the town was forced to improve the provision for waste disposal and sewerage purification. Diseases such as typhus were rampant at that time. A treatment works was built on Entwistle Road to

where tubs of deodorised waste matter, collected from around the town at night, were taken. No matter how many improvements were made or how many less people were suffering from diseases caused by poor health facilities, the council could not stand still and the public health system had to be constantly developed. An indication of progress can be seen in the number of houses with pail closets. In 1906 there were 16,400 and only 900 in 1955.

The first public lavatories were built in 1907 on Cheetham Street and soon there were six more. The Entwistle Road works became a refuse disposal plant in 1937 where, what must have been the pioneering work of separating and reclaiming all marketable salvage like paper, textiles, tins, metals and bottles, was begun. A public campaign to highlight this work was also established. All waste products were incinerated, giving heat to boilers, thus providing all the steam required at the adjoining public baths as well as to heat and power the plant itself. The need for greater efficiency lead to the acquisition of petrol driven vehicles including Model T Ford vans. This enabled the council to deal with the ever increasing problem of providing a public health service which met current needs.

Continued overleaf

The Entwistle Road plant remained in operation until the 1960s when it was burnt down. The problems caused by using coal for heat and power resulted in the establishment of the nearby Naithlands tip off Milnrow Road where dust and clinkers were taken and an overhead pulley was introduced to move the waste.

After 1925 galvanised iron dustbins were

introduced and by 1948 the corporation was providing and maintaining standard dustbins for all domestic users. An interesting observation was made in 1955 that the streets themselves were becoming much cleaner due in the main to 'the almost total elimination of the horse' at work on the roads.

Expansion of the street cleaning service was a necessity as the number of cars and vehicles on the roads increased and the amount of litter from packaging and newspapers also grew. By 1955 petrol driven engines were acquired to empty the town's 14,000 gullies.

The council had also bought nine snow ploughs and eight gritting machines. However, it became obvious that 'the man on the beat' was still regarded as best for the job of keeping the streets clean and each road man was responsible for his own patch dealing with this problem of more and more litter. The number of streets in Rochdale had doubled between 1900 and 1955 while the population had grown at an even greater pace. Rochdale foresaw the need for an efficient cleansing service and that paved the way for the work which is still carried on in the town.

"We're only doing it for the kids" would be the view of the adults as the children of Clover Hall Crescent are treated to a tea party to celebrate the end of the war in Europe. So the tables were set out, chairs found from a variety of sources, tablecloths pressed and mams and grans with an occasional grandad, set out to entertain these smiling children, with maybe in this time of shortage potted meat sandwiches, jelly, buns and pop. A victory cake would more than likely have been baked and decorated in red, white and blue. Afterwards on this sunny day in May 1945, games would be played, races would be run and the worries of air raids and bombs would be over and all it needed now is for dads and brothers and uncles to come safely home from the war. The town of Rochdale had earlier taken a little time to come to terms with the news that Germany had surrendered. This was known on Monday, May 7th and officially announced to the nation the following day. The people of the town had gathered in front of the Town Hall to hear the news and gradually the town began to outwardly celebrate peace at least in Europe but not in the Far East. Bunting began to appear on shops and businesses and on houses. Red, white and blue appeared everywhere, even in some places painted on kerbstones. On the Wednesday and the following evenings crowds gathered again in front of the Town Hall. There was dancing to a gramophone and on that first night boys from the High School formed a protective merry-go-round type circle round the dancers. Milnrow Public Band played until 10pm with the Town Hall illuminated until midnight. Naturally everyone was glad and relieved the war was over and could celebrate the coming of peace. They were determined to enjoy themselves in their own way but it all appeared to have been in good humour and as one report stated at the time there was 'no public mafficking'.

Left: Rochdale's most famous lady, Gracie Fields, signs autographs at St. Thomas's School, New Hey watched by the Chief Constable, Mr F S Gale and the Deputy, Mr S Walker. 'Our Gracie' had been to the school to the October 1963 concert given by Rochdale Borough Police Concert Party in aid of Milnrow Old People's Welfare Committee. At the end she had given her thanks in song with the audience joining in enthusiastically and then received a bouquet from the oldest person there, 92 year old Mrs Elizabeth Pearson. Gracie's own trophy was won by Inspector Dennis Butterworth in charge of the Concert Party who had got out of his sick bed to be present. To his complete surprise Gracie's husband, Boris, also received a present on his 60th birthday of Lancashire cotton towels from Mr Gale. A gatecrasher had surprised everyone by pretending to be a press photographer when all local actor, Charles Starley, wanted to do was to meet Gracie. Earlier she had attended the annual meeting of the Rochdale branch of the N.S.P.C.C and proposed the re-election of officers in song, 'Scarlet Ribbons'. Born in a modest house in Molesworth Street, Gracie Fields became a household name in this country and a Hollywood star but she never forgot her home town and its citizens, her true fans. She always said her proudest moment was when she received the Freedom of the Borough in 1937 and the town's celebrations of the centenary of her

birth in 1898 are a fitting tribute to her.

Above: The importance of being an able communicator in front of the television screen is vital for any politician these days. To be an aspiring male politician you need a ' high profile' wife. The Liberal candidate for Rochdale in the 1958 by-election had those. He was television personality, Ludovic Kennedy. His wife was Moira Shearer, a famous ballerina and the star of the film 'The Red Shoes'. He also received active support from another television household name, Robin Day and from the party leader, Jo Grimond. Manchester based, Granada T.V. lead the way and staged two 'meet the candidates' debates. The B.B.C. came next and interviewed members of the public outside the Town Hall. Even a television crew from the United States got in on the act and for the first ever time in this country an election appeared in such a manner on television. Think back to the 1997 and earlier elections and how much time, money and effort was spent saturating the viewers with election news, views and trivia. For the record the Labour candidate, John (Jack) McCann gained the seat for Labour with Kennedy 4500 votes behind. Because of an old agreement with the Conservatives this was the first time voters had been given an opportunity to vote for the Liberals so Kennedy's was a good effort and paved the way for Rochdale's famous Liberal M.P., Cyril Smith.

Above: The youngest party ever shown was the title given to the children of the primary department of New Hey County School on their visit in July 1964 to Rochdale Fire Station in Duncan Street. Station Officer Burrows has to give this young man his own fireman's lift in order that he can explain the purpose of the blue flashing light.

The smiling children and their equally happy looking teacher would been shown the control room, the four fire appliances, all the equipment like ladders and hoses and helmets and axes and the famous pole and all the other things which made children think being a fireman would be a wonderful life.

For them the visit will have been eagerly looked forward to and one they would find exciting in their own way.

They would each take with them afterwards their own memory of the visit and the teacher would aim to bring those experiences together at school into a kind of collective scrapbook to which every child will have contributed.

Not for them hopefully a test at the end to see what they have remembered but a bank of drawings and writings and some drama and a talk in assembly to the rest of the school. That is what makes school the happiest days of your life - to look back and say 'I can remember the day we went to the fire station. It was great.'

Right: The Easter Bank Holiday weekend proved to be a very cold and wet one for these visitors to Hollingworth Lake in 1964. The first holiday weekend of the year was traditionally the time for the Weighvers Seaport to receive hundreds of visitors and extra buses were not full by any means and traffic, unusually, was able to move freely on Halifax Road. Traders stated there were more visitors on an ordinary Sunday. The busiest place was the fair. This inland seaside resort had been developed to provide for visitors with pleasure gardens, cafes and hotels in order to provide an alternative to Blackpool on Rochdale's doorstep. Activities on the lake, built as an giant reservoir in the nineteenth century, included sailing and rowing regattas and fishing and it had continued to attract every year thousands of visitors. Although the numbers at the lake were disappointing compared to other years, there is, looking at the photograph, a large number of them which does give an indication of how popular the resort was. They are well wrapped up for the weather in headscarves and coats. One or two of the gentlemen's hairstyles will jog the memory and the leisure wear craze has certainly not caught on. For the record the coldest day was Good Friday with a maximum temperature of 41 degrees Fahrenheit, with the highest all Bank Holiday of 45 degrees. As one trader remarked ' You can't expect any better when Easter falls in March!

Above: A very youthful Queen Elizabeth lit up the platform of Rochdale Railway Station when she arrived there in 1954 as part of an extensive tour of the northern mill towns of Lancashire.

Her Majesty, accompanied by the Duke of Edinburgh, was greeted by the Mayor of Rochdale and a party of civic officials before setting off to engagements in the town. Crowds of loyal and enthusiastic Rochdale subjects lined the route, cheering and waving flags as the popular Royal couple passed by.

Right: A more natural picture of the Queen and the Duke of Edinburgh would be difficult to imagine. The delightful image was captured by Rochdale's most accomplished photographer, Clifford C Ashton, in 1954 and shows the Royal couple in a relaxed mood aboard the Royal train. This was the moment before the train left Rochdale Station after the couple's visit to the town. Lord and Lady Derby can be seen standing on the platform, Lady Derby looking stylish in her sleek mink coat, and her husband barely concealing the smile which suggests that everything had gone exactly to plan.

The 1955 inspection of the Borough's Police Force was conducted by Major Armstrong here in front of the Town Hall which acted as police headquarters at this time. Lined up ready for inspection are P.C.s Ogden, Hamer and Cooper with their dogs and behind, looking like C.I.D. men, are Detectives Porrit, Breese, Jones, Plane, Stables and Gladstone. Accompanying Her Majesty's Inspector is the Chief Constable who would have proudly let him know how the police service was being expanded to cope with the increasing current demands. The establishment of a dog section was one. A Single Fingerprint Bureau had been set up with one Detective Inspector liaising with Headquarters. Cadets were to undergo a more systematic and rigorous training programme because, whereas in the past recruits would have undergone some kind of military training prior to joining the force, this was not necessarily the case then. The number of vehicles had been increased to include nine cars, two vans and five motor-cycles, each equipped with a two-way radio linked to a communications room. The introduction of policewomen on the beat was regarded as a success and it was announced they were responsible for 15 arrests that year. These developments were a reaction to the expansion in the duties of the police and the increase in the number of crimes committed, especially by juveniles. There had been an increase in the number of 999 calls but the Chief Constable could report that the use of knuckle-dusters had declined. The rise in the number of traffic accidents was a concern with danger spots being on Manchester Road on the part between Duster Avenue and Law Street and on Oldham Road at the junction of Kingsway and Crawford Street and also at White Rake Gardens.

Around the town centre

This is a very early 1900s photograph of the area around what is now Newgate and before the bridging of the River Roch. The well-dressed gentlemen are clearly waiting to enter Dawsons before it moved to new premises rather than Yates's Wine Lodge which later was re-sited further up Newgate to where it stands now. What cannot be seen on the left side of the building is the traditional Yates's sign advertising the company's 'Honesty, Excellence and Purity' The first lodge was opened in Oldham in 1884 by a Lancashire wine merchant, Peter Yates, and the Rochdale one was not long to follow. He stated his simple objective was to make people happier and healthier and based the simple

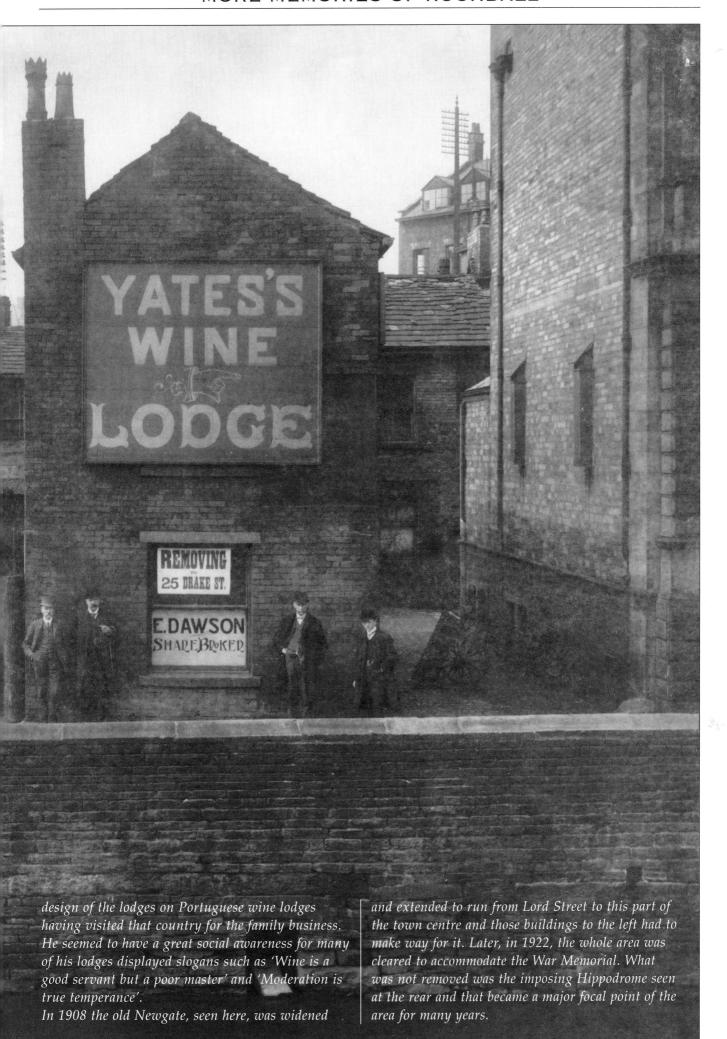

design of the lodges on Portuguese wine lodges
having visited that country for the family business.
He seemed to have a great social awareness for many
of his lodges displayed slogans such as 'Wine is a
good servant but a poor master' and 'Moderation is
true temperance'.
In 1908 the old Newgate, seen here, was widened
and extended to run from Lord Street to this part of
the town centre and those buildings to the left had to
make way for it. Later, in 1922, the whole area was
cleared to accommodate the War Memorial. What
was not removed was the imposing Hippodrome seen
at the rear and that became a major focal point of the
area for many years.

Above: More like a stately home than a bank, especially with the horse and carriage awaiting outside, the Midland Bank at the corner of Yorkshire Street and The Butts gives the air of financial and architectural permanence. It was one of many banks in the area which came to the town as Rochdale's industrial prosperity grew. Even as late as 1960 there were at least seven banks in this part of town with names like the Yorkshire Penny, Martins and Westminster. The financial world has changed since those days. Banks had a cathedral-like air to them as though money and business was sacred. They were almost male preserves of men in dark suits, with grills at the counter and everyone seeming to speak in hushed tones and the tellers appearing to know more than they were 'telling'. Compare that to the openness, bustle and relative informality of today's institutions where even the traditional building societies, established as friendly societies for the well-being of the local community, are now national and even international and where as long as you are a good or a prospective customer you are made to feel welcome. However, although practices have changed and more people take advantage of the increase in the number of services on offer, like mortgages and insurance, buildings like the Midland Bank do give an air of permanence and stability and do enhance the town centre where other changes may not.

Right: The advantage of building a 445 metre bridge covering the River Roch was that it prevented any large scale building development in this part of the town, hence the relative calm at any part of the day. All the bridge had was to withstand the local transport system of trams and buses and the steady growth of private and commercial vehicles. Here this early 1960s photograph looking towards Smith Street from the Butts gives a clear indication of this ease of pedestrian and motor traffic. There were about 10 bus shelters in this part of the town as the corporation transport system used this as the town centre terminus and those familiar diesel engined omnibuses, first introduced in 1932, with their blue and ivory livery made Rochdale the envy of other near-by towns for the efficiency and the economy of the system. What was needed was a bus station which would be accessible for vehicle and passenger alike, which would not cause traffic jams and, probably, which would be reasonably cheap to build, It was not long before that bus station was a reality when Kelsall and Kemps Mills just beyond the Regal Cinema were demolished in 1962, followed later by the old market to make way for a whole package of redevelopment including the much needed bus station, new municipal offices and a highly visible multi-storey car park.

This really is an evocative photograph showing the Town Hall in all its splendour. The open areas around it have a history of parades and processions, some dramatic, some joyous and all memorable. Behind stands the Parish Church dedicated to St Chad and, as we come down the 122 steps to Packer Street, we see the Flying Horse, the Empire Cinema, the Central Hotel and the County Court before Fleece Street is reached. Behind these is the Municipal High School for Boys and on the same site is the Technical School. Opposite the Town Hall is the grand Post Office building and to its left the Memorial Gardens and the Sir Edward Lutyens designed Cenotaph on the site of the Manor House or as it was also better known as, the Orchard. The Hippodrome is at the end of Newgate and opposite on Lord Street is Pioneer House. The still existing Salvation Army Citadel stands on Lord Street near its junction with Blackwater Street and Newgate. To the right is Toad Lane stretching from St Mary's Church, Wardleworth to Lord Street and almost parallel is Yorkshire Street, the old pack horse route to Halifax and the premier shopping area of the town. At the bottom are the many banks centred around this street, the Butts and South Parade and equally as many public houses. The old streets and lanes around here such as The Walk, Stationers Entry, The Butts Avenue, Baillie Street and Lyceum Passage will no doubt bring back recollections of work and business and of shopping and entertainment as they are still vital parts of the life of the town

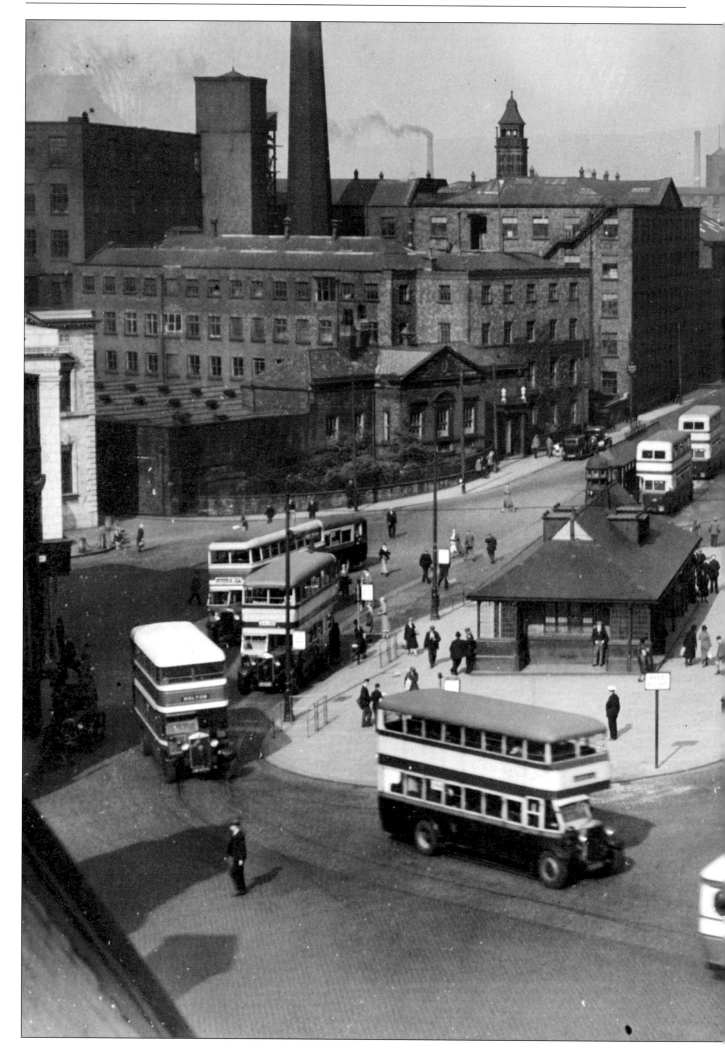

Are the buses driving the wrong way round the island as they head off from the town centre? There must have been a good reason! Apart from that this photograph gives a very clear view of the area before the changes to which have occurred over the past 30 years or so. Butts House, the next door offices of Kelsall and Kemp Butts Mill, has yet to give way to the Regal cinema. As we move further along Duncan Street, the Fire Station tower stands above the Mills and across the road is Electric House. Coming back, the Wellington Hotel retains a prominent place at the corner of Drake Street. That sight changed very little over the years except that the bus shelters were moved to the sides of the road, thus making the catching of a bus a less hazardous exercise. Changes there were, however, and someone returning to Rochdale would look at the other side of the road and have some difficulty in remembering where everything was. At least there are identifiable landmarks like the Wellington, even though it is 'Bojangles', and Electric House, now another mundane council office. The importance of providing a bus station was self-evident for no matter how convenient it was to have your bus drop you off or pick you up close to shops and offices, the increase in private and commercial traffic during the last 20 years made that inevitable.

Above: A rare sight of a policeman on point-duty directing traffic into Drake Street just after trams had given way to trolley-buses in 1932, although the tracks and overhead lines remain. In view of the fact that only one car needs directing the policeman looks under-employed and pedestrians seem to be able to walk to and from the bus shelters without too much trouble. Obviously there was no need for the Green Cross Code in the 1930s. The familiar frontage of Burton's 'Tailor of Taste' stands out to the right of the photograph. It is interesting to note that Burton's would be one of the few shops in the area at that time and probably the largest. In keeping with its policy of moving with the times, Burton's changed all it shop frontages in the 1960s, the only trouble being they lost their uniqueness and looked like any other High Street trader. At this time the Post Office had recently been built.

Below: Today very little appears to have changed around the area of Wet Rake Gardens. Should you stand where Oldham Road meets School Lane, Drake Street, Milnrow Road and George Street, the sights you would see would almost be the same apart from the roads being so much busier. The gardens themselves now contain a car-park on close inspection. The offices of the 'Rochdale Observer' are still situated on the left hand side of Drake Street. The 'Observer', established in 1856, has survived where other papers like the 'Sentinel', 'Times' and 'Star and Recorder' have not and although it has lost its true independence, it still manages to be a local paper reflecting local news and views rather than being an off-shoot of a near-by big city. What cannot be seen properly in this photograph behind the 'Observer' is the Carlton Ballroom, opened in 1934 as a purpose built dance hall. At this time it had succumbed to the Bingo craze but recently has been restored to its former glory and patrons old and new, young and not so young, can dance the night away in wonderful surroundings. Further down Drake Street is the Champness Hall built in 1925 by local Methodists as a mission hall but because of its spaciousness and grandeur a suitable venue at this time for great occasions like school speech days.

This mid-1960s photograph gives a clear picture of this part of the town prior to redevelopment. On the left is the William Deacon's Bank and next to it the A.B.C. Cinema formerly the Regal and now reverted to Regal with 'Moon' added to it and dedicated to Bingo. Behind the cinema are the old Public Health offices. Kelsall and Kemps Mill has gone and that affords us a good view of Hardmans Mill and to the left are the firemen's houses and stables and Duncan Street Fire Station itself. Jennings Mill and the tax office bring up the rear, the latter to many a person's dismay at the time had recently survived a fire.

All that area has now been redeveloped to

provide Municipal Offices, bus station and car park and the Wheatsheaf Centre which opens out on to Yorkshire Street.

At the bottom right is Fleece Street which has changed little over the years and this part of the town contains many buildings part of the town's past and very much worth preserving.

Interestingly enough a Golden Fleece is part of the town's coat of arms and was also part of the badge on the green blazers of pupils of the Secondary School. In the bottom right hand corner stands what was the Central School and at the corner of Fleece Street and Drake Street are the then Borough Education Offices.

Standing today on St Mary's Gate and looking towards the Exchange Shopping centre one has to think very hard about what used to be there. What were the names of the streets? Which mill was here? What was the name of the church? There used to be a cinema somewhere here and a pub and a workman's' club. These photographs are a kind of 'half way house' between what used to be and what is going to happen when Blackwater Street and Lord Street are wiped off the map. The former, as we look at these late 1960s views, is still a thoroughfare as cars turn into St Mary's Gate but the land on what will become a dual carriageway is beginning to be cleared. Looking down the left of the street are familiar ex-landmarks, like the Unitarian Church and the Old Clock Face and the one building which just had to survive, the Pioneers Co-operative Store, and beyond the store the comforting sight of the Clock Tower of the Town Hall. As this lady strides up St Mary's Gate past the lorry carrying the wicker skips, a not so familiar sight these days, towards the junction with Albert Street and on to College Street and Spotland Road, she could look towards Manchester Road, just before it turns into Lord Street, at the clearances taking place. Gone already is the Pavilion Cinema and Brierley's Mills is to become the site of the new College.

The telephone exchange in front of the mills does manage to survive. Rochdale here is becoming redeveloped and there has to be a price to pay in the name of progress and that is understandable. There would be areas in any industrial town which grew as rapidly as Rochdale where they had outlived their usefulness or where it would not be reasonable for people to live and developing them becomes a vital necessity. Other needs have taken over, hence housing estates, large car parks, ring roads, one-way systems and shopping centres, Therefore town centres have had to be re-defined. What is special and unique about any town ought be cherished and preserved in order to retain its character and there are many buildings and many parts of this town worthy of that.

Rochdale in 1969 is in the midst of change and this photograph gives a clear indication what is happening to the town. The new can be seen in the College and the high rise flats on St. Mary's Gate now acting as a ring road where College Street and Manchester Road used to meet Lord Street. Then it merges with the old St Mary's Gate at the top of the picture. Rochdale Cricket Field will soon give way to a supermarket and electrical store and at the cross-roads of St Mary's Gate and the Esplanade is the Trinity Church now replaced by a funeral parlour. Across the road stands Broadfield Park and the Broadfield Hotel, formerly a nurses' home and opposite is the Rochdale library containing these days only the excellent Local Studies Section and the Art gallery. The rest of the facilities have moved to the Wheatsheaf Centre. Behind the library the land around Blackwater Street and Lord Street on the Holme, site of Rochdale's traditional fair, is being cleared to make way for the new courts and a new shopping centre which was to be built in two phases in 1975 and 1976, called originally the Rochdale Shopping Centre and now the Exchange containing not only shops but a covered market. What can be seen is the old Pioneers Store at the bottom of Toad Lane which was then a much longer street than it is now as it winds its way from St Mary's Gate to Lord Street. The Esplanade, containing the Post Office and the 'finest Town Hall in the north of England', leads on to South Parade and the Butts where at the junction with Yorkshire Street it becomes the fulcrum of the town's commercial life. Centred around here are the banks, the shops and the offices and here we can see evidence of change as the land which used to be Kelsall and Kemps in front of Hardman's Mill has been cleared and it will not be long before the covered market next to it is to be re-developed.

The Rialto, pronounced locally 'Rye-alto' rather than the Venetian 'Ree-alto', opened in 1928 at the junction of School Lane and Drake Street and, with the adjoining cafe, it was noted for its Venetian decor, hence the name. The cinema was built by local craftsmen and was palace-like with its terra cotta exterior, marble floors and staircases, polished mahogany panels and elaborate paintwork, including scenes from Healey Dell. Patrons would experience all electric heating and ventilation and sit in any one of the 1874 upholstered seats. The Rank Organisation became the cinema's owner in the 1950s and removed the original orchestra pit and dressing rooms and because of less demand reduced the seating capacity to 500. A far cry this from the Rialto's golden days when it was rare for seats to be available in all parts of the cinema.

Rank decided to close the Odeon in 1975 and set a closing date of 15th November but a fire, which damaged the screen meant, it closed for business two weeks earlier and Rochdale lost one of its great assets. After closure various plans and suggestions were put forward for its future use, including one to re-open it as a cinema by a company which had boxer Billy Walker associated with it. Other ideas put forward and come to nought were for it to become a skate-board arena just as that craze was dying out, another was a roller skating rink and in 1979 two local 13 year olds, Anna Donadio and Eva Skierka, wanted it to become a sports centre for the town's youth. Instead the Odeon joined the Empire and the Kings Cinemas and offered the town more Bingo, until it suffered its final indignity in February 1981 when it was badly damaged by fire.

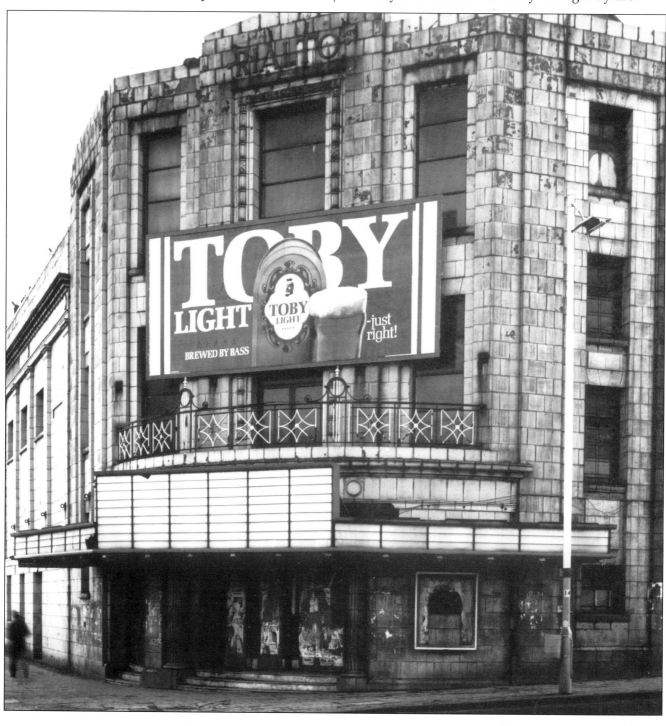

Flash, bang, wallop – what a picture!

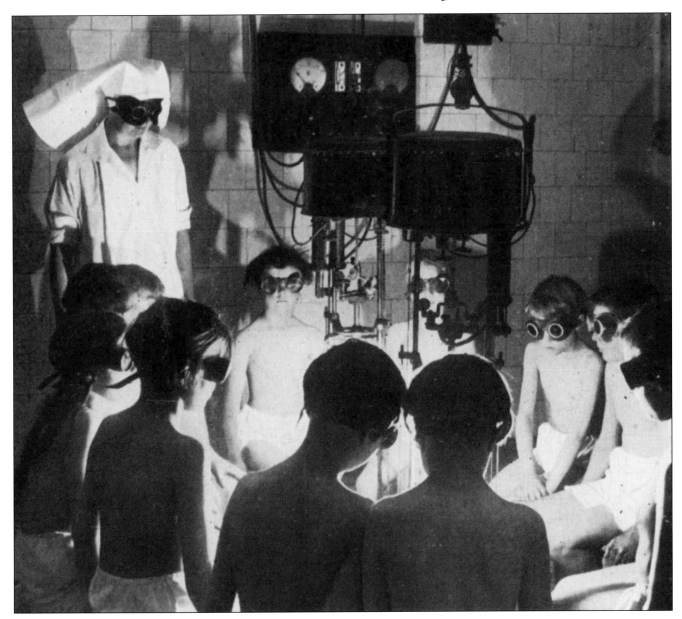

What looks to be a weird ritual is in fact children receiving ultra violet or 'artificial sunlight' treatment at Rochdale Infirmary. This practice was not unique to Rochdale or in many other towns and cities in this country in the 1920s and 30s. This treatment was considered vital in the build-up of Vitamin D as an aid to bone growth in developing children. It is estimated that over 23000 received that treatment in 1928 with children from the open-air school at Brownhill receiving it regularly, some as often as once a week. This type of school for children considered *delicate,* which usually meant chest problems, was one of a series of measures that were adopted to ensure that children lead healthier lives than those of previous generations. Hence the development of the school meals service, milk at playtime, orange juice from the clinic, cod liver oil of malt, halibut oil capsules and a whole range of other measures. The list of services which the NHS Trusts provide today in connection with child development is wide, ranging from ante-natal care to infant food sales to school nurses and child health clinics and to young persons' health centres. The care of the young is still an issue but it has different emphases these days. In the 1920s it was about making children healthy enough to live. Now it is more about leading and maintaining a healthy life-style.

Left: The morning of 21st December 1963 proved to be very busy for Rochdale police as they had to deal with two traffic accidents. The first in the very early hours involved a double-decker bus and a mini-van colliding at Shawclough. The caption which accompanied the photograph in the newspaper showing the Kingsway bus and the van squaring up to each other was 'Dignity with Impudence' The second accident occurred at 10.25am when the number two Healey bus and a Thames trader van, belonging to Hogan and Harding of Manchester, carrying rubble, collided in Shawclough Road, near Bentley Street. The lorry came off worse as its petrol tank was fractured and the Fire Brigade had to be called out to wash away the petrol. The bus which, fortunately, was carrying no passengers at the time, was also extensively damaged. The vehicles were travelling in the opposite direction when the collision took place and both hit the wall belonging to Turner Brothers Asbestos Company and caused a great deal of damage to it. The driver of the lorry, Mr. Joseph Kuteba, sustained a foot injury, while the bus driver, Mr. John Brian Callaghan, and the conductor, Mr. M. Kennedy Dawson, were treated for shock. In view of the damage to the vehicles, the wall and the telegraph pole it must have been quite a crash.

Above: What proved to be a very expensive way to spend a penny occurred to James Taylor of Ripponden near Halifax when he parked his lorry at the top of Willbutts Lane to go to the toilet for then it 'took off' down the hill. What happened next if it were a film would cause a few laughs. It was not so funny for two motorists coming up the hill. Mrs Doris Clow's mini-van was struck. Behind her in his Vauxhall Estate, waiting 'for his last moment' was how he later described it, was Mr Harold Horsfall of Norden. Fortunately, the lorry, owned by Claude Hellowell & Sons, only gave it a glancing blow and, accelerating all the time, ran on. A lamp standard and a 'Keep Left ' bollard were next in its line before the lorry met its end at the corner of Rooley Street and Edenfield Street. Mrs Hilda Wild was upstairs at her home at 22 Edenfield Street when she heard a bang and the sound of glass breaking. To her utter amazement there was the lorry in her hallway and behind was a trail of damage and mayhem. Fortunately no-one was injured apart from a startled Mrs Wild, who was treated for shock, and two relieved motorists. Mr Taylor would certainly remember the day he wished he had not wanted to respond to nature's call and, despite its abrupt stop, the lorry was reversed out under its own steam.

Above: There will be a time in may people's lives when they think back to an incident or situation in which they were involved and just cringe at the thought of it. Perhaps Wasyl Kuczarawskj had that feeling. It had been a good night out with friends and as he made his way home to Spotland Bridge he felt happy enough to sing something from 'Orpheus in the Underworld'. It was not long after that two youths could hear that music coming from deep down a gutter and there they found Waysl down the grid and up to his armpits in dirty water two feet below the level of the road. Three policeman could not get him out. The Fire Brigade could not move him. The emergency works squad of Rochdale Corporation, equipped with a pneumatic drill, arrived and as Wasyl kept singing, workmen and firemen on this October night in 1966 tore away at the pavement to release him, with a 14lb sledgehammer just inches away from his head. Finally Wasyl came out of the grid like, as described by a policeman, 'a cork out of a bottle'. He then replaced the grill and, still singing, was taken to hospital where he was treated for exposure. Was it one of those nights you wish to erase from your memory? Wasyl's last official words on the matter give a clue. 'You might as well sing as be miserable'.

Left: Four year old Alison Jane Smith would remember 11th October 1963 for a long time when she got more than she bargained for after buying a penny lolly on her way to Meanwood Infants School. When she took off the wrapper, she lifted the grill of a drain in the school playground to put the paper down. Then catastrophe struck. Her left foot slipped down the hole and was wedged under the lip of a stone drainpipe. The caretaker unsuccessfully tried to free her by rubbing the foot with grease. The headmistress, Miss C.M.Wilson, called for the Fire Brigade. Firemen, however, could not remove her shoe so it was decided to dig under the drain. By this time Alison' mum, Marjorie, Auntie Vera and Uncle Bob and cousin Alan had arrived. Alison by now was very worried not at being stuck but at the state of her sock because that self-same aunt and uncle were coming to tea next Sunday and that sock would need a wash. After two hours of patiently chipping away at the thick layer of concrete, several bricks and a mound of earth, Fireman Alan Bevington finally got his reward and Alison, her foot covered in oil, was pulled free. 'The little marvel', as the firemen termed her, was uninjured but to be on the safe side a police car whisked her and mam to Rochdale Infirmary for a check-up. And what was Alison sucking in the car? A lollipop of course.

If your mam or dad or both worked at Foxcroft Mill in 1963 and you were under the age of nine then you were invited to the firm's children's Christmas party organised by a committee established for that purpose. On 28th December you put on your party clothes and set off for Littleborough Conservative Club to meet 84 other children. There you would play loads of games like 'pass the parcel' and 'musical chairs' and then have a special Christmas tea with sandwiches, cakes, jelly, ice-cream and lemonade. Then you play more games until it was time for the great man to arrive.

While you were waiting for him, a photographer would come to take your picture and you would show how much you were enjoying it with a big smile and a shout and show off your balloon if you were lucky enough to have one. Then you and all the other children form a large circle and HE arrives, Father Christmas that is. Each of you is given a gift and at the end there is a carrier bag for you to take home and it is filled with fruits and chocolate.

And what did the children aged between nine and thirteen do?

Well, they went to the circus at a later date!

The story of the Rochdale Pioneers is here being filmed in 1969 in the street where the Co-operative movement originated. The history of its birth, now well documented, was not as well known outside this part of the world for many years. The co-op was taken almost for granted without enough people knowing the circumstances which decided those Pioneers to take this action or their struggle to initially make it work or the rapid growth of the movement when it did begin to prosper. What is left of Toad Lane now after town centre redevelopment is little and even in this photograph the site of the original main store is just an empty space. At least now there is a visible reminder of the origins of the movement. The little shop at 33 Toad Lane, seen here, opened its doors on the 21st December 1844. It has been acquired by the Co-operative Union and converted into a museum. Visitors on first entering are struck by its lay out. There is a basic simplicity about the place as in the original store when the goods sold were few in number. On the walls is a poster which sets out the famous Rochdale Principles, the basis of the movement, which state emphatically the need for open membership, democratic control and political and religious neutrality. Toad Lane itself is now part of a conservation area and attracts visitors from all over the world.

'One arch started to go, then another and then the rest went. They all went down in slow motion like a ripple of cards' is how explosions expert, Mervyn Simpson, described the unexplained collapse of the arches in this 104 year old Roch Valley railway viaduct on the Rochdale to Bacup line. A teatime walk in July 1972 for Alec and Ralph Crossley and their sister Marie proved to be a dangerous adventure as they were on the next arches as they began to fall. Little Joanne Powell had to be pulled clear by her father as she stood underneath in the fields trying to get a good view when instead of the one arch collapsing under the force of the dynamite, the next 11 went also with a great roar amid clouds of smoke. Stones and debris crashed down on Entwistle Street and the bravery of P C Charles Reader who fortunately was in his panda car in the street at this rush hour time when he realised what was happening, prevented a serious situation arising. He immediately parked the car under the Entwistle arch, stood in the midst of it all and stopped the traffic. There was awful damage to houses from falling stones and debris and from collapsed chimney pots on to roofs and local residents likened the tremor to an earthquake. So much rubble fell into the river that it became swollen to three times its normal depth. The water and gas mains underneath the road were broken and the surrounding areas were without water for the next 12 hours. The electricity was cut off because of the danger of a gas leak and that meant only one thing for 2000 people of Entwistle Street, Oswald Street, and Arthington Street - they had to evacuate their homes. This had turned into an emergency. What happened next, in the words of one observer, 'was farcical'. No-one would accept responsibility for what was left of the bridge. Was it the council's? Or the demolition contractor's? Or the free-lance explosives expert's? Indecision meant delay. The 'man from the ministry' was called in. He took charge and the viaduct was made safe during the following days without any more explosions, much to the relief of people like Fred Biddulph and his wife who had slept that first eventful night in their car. Soon they were all allowed to return to their homes. What caused the collapse? Too much explosive? The poor state of the stonework? Those questions tasked the mind of the officials. For people like the Crossleys, the Powells and the Biddulphs they were just pleased to get back to their homes with only a close escape.

On the move

Pantomimes have been for a long time a Christmas tradition in this country. They require a handsome male lead, played by a long legged actress, a beautiful female lead, a villain to hiss at, a comedian or two, sometimes in drag, a cow or a cat, a good fairy and nasty witch, lots of jokes, the come-uppence at the end for the villain and a happy ever after ending. Other frills could be attached depending on which pantomime was being performed so it was a bit of a break in tradition for the Palace Theatre in Manchester to present for its 1963/4 production 'Peter Pan On Ice'. An ice show was not a new venture for that theatre but not as a pantomime. So the Darling family and Captain Hook would on this occasion be skaters. This innovation did not deter audiences from attending for the tradition of an annual visit had to be maintained and so Mrs. M. Cattlin, Milnrow Spinning Company's Welfare Officer organised this one to the Palace Theatre on 28th December 1963 for employees' children, accompanied by six adults. In the days before television played such a major part in the lives of all of us, especially children, the sight of real-life performers would have been regarded with awe and to see an ice show with a great deal of wonder. Hopefully these children and their parents felt that way after their visit.

Above: It took three double decker buses, each bearing the company's famous logo, to transport these children to see Peter Pan On Ice'. Dunlop Cotton Mills, at one time the world's largest factory under one roof with a complex of spinning and weaving sheds spread over 33 acres, needed this number because in February 1964 it was still one of the town's biggest employers. The company was large enough to have a thriving social section so during the interval at the Manchester Palace Theatre these children can look forward to an ice-cream and afterwards as a parting gift a bag of fruit and sweets. This treat would have been in addition to the children's Christmas party featuring games, tea and a children's entertainer. The organisation for all these events was in the hands of the company's Welfare Manager, Mr. Dayard Grimshaw, himself renowned as a part-time magician. Dunlop had a thriving social club for its employees and ran the Dunlop Dynamos Football team. The highlight of the year was the staff dance at the Carlton Ballroom. This all took place at the beginning of the end of an era as the demand for Lancashire cotton suddenly declined after over one hundred years of growth and mills had to close or, like Dunlop, reduce in size. Economies had to be made and employees' welfare provision as such gave way to survival as the struggle to compete for markets for cotton intensified.

Inset: A visit to Manchester Airport was the first port of call for these children as they waited eagerly to board the coach outside Ellen Smith's on Newgate. The parent's committee of the Roch Nursing and Ambulance Cadet Divisions of the St John's Ambulance Brigade had organised this outing which was planned to later go on to Southport. Perhaps it would be the first time these children had ever been to an airport although that probably could not be said about the many children of the same age today. So packed sandwiches to the ready, a bit of spending money, best clothes on, which means to a couple of lads their school uniform, and off these smiling children and parents went. Manchester, however, lived up to its reputation. The weather at the airport let them down. That outside viewing area turned out to be too cold and the rain, which eventually came, cut short their stay there. The visit to Southport took place earlier than planned but, fortunately, the children and the adults enjoyed better weather. The rain stayed away, the sun came out and, although it remained quite breezy, they had a full afternoon and evening at the seaside and would come home remembering the attractions of Southport in September 1964 rather than a cold viewing area at Ringway, despite the thrill of seeing the large passenger planes heading to and coming from places only read about in Geography books.

Above: Whittle's Bakery of Littleborough were bread wholesalers from the 1890s until the firm was sold to Allied Bakeries in 1957. Henry Whittle started the firm with a horse-driven handcart and after he died it was run by the Butterworth side of the family. By 1930 the bakery was in its heyday working a 24 hour, three shift system delivering its own bread, including the famous Purity Eight, over a twenty mile radius even to West Yorkshire in these vans which always had a young delivery boy accompanying the driver. The practice of using a cart to deliver bread locally was kept up, however. The firm built houses for its employees on appropriately named Whittle Street, a practice not unknown in the days of industrial expansion. These red-bricked, two-up and two-down houses were allocated on the basis that the more humble your position in the bakery, the closer to it you lived. The foreman lived in the large house at the far end. Whittles had its own sports ground including a cricket field and pavilion. No doubt the enthusiasm for that came from one of the Butterworth family who was good enough to have played for Lancashire and the bakery itself seemed to have had an uncanny knack of recruiting to its staff employees who were good cricketers.

Right: The lady and gentleman outside the Regal cinema on this day in 1958 could either be waiting for a bus, for this part of the town acted as a terminus in those days or they are the beginning of a queue to enter the cinema. The Regal had been built in 1938 on the site of The Butts House, used as offices by Kelsall and Kemps, and the first film ever shown there was 'Stella Dallas' starring the American actress Barbara Stanwyck. If that couple were going the cinema on this day, they may have been going to watch the very popular romantic comedy 'Breakfast at Tiffany's' with Audrey Hepburn as the female lead in which she sang the much recorded song 'Moon River' sung better on disc later by Danny Williams. At one time Rochdale could boast 11 cinemas, the first being the Old Circus later called the Hippodrome and now it has none. Cinema going in 1958 was a popular leisure activity and with such great films at that period such as 'Doctor Zhivago' starring Julie Christie and Omar Sharif, the stirring 'Bridge Over The River Kwai' and the musical 'West Side Story' all having been shown prior to this time. Audiences flocked to the cinema, bought their popcorn and winegums, followed the usherette's torch which never seemed to have enough shine, settled down in their seats, watch a Donald Duck and Goofy cartoon, Pathe News, advertisements extolling the virtues of a shop not far from this cinema and then lived in the world of the big film for the next hour or so.

Left: This photograph speaks for itself. Master Douglas Will of Market Street Shawforth is ready for his 1964 Wakes Week holiday and stands on Rochdale Station equipped for a seaside vacation, dressed in his best, watch on to ensure the train goes on time and leaves behind a deserted town as Rochdale decamps itself to the Lancashire coastal resorts. It was once said, no doubt with tongue in cheek, that if you wanted a loaf of bread in Rochdale during Wakes you had to go to Oldham for it. It was also said, rather cynically, that Wakes was the annual reminder of how dirty was the normal atmosphere of your home town. Not that Douglas seems to care about that when he has other things on his mind. The train journey has to be enjoyed first, the return to last year's boarding house with the same fierce landlady, the donkey rides, the funfairs, staying up late, sandcastles, rock, fish and chips, even a cold sea, even calamine lotion on a sore red back and many more things beside. Why go elsewhere? There was a freedom about a seaside holiday worth parents saving up for in the savings club, buying the railway ticket in advance because the station would be congested and generally forgetting about work for one or even two whole weeks.

Below: The Green Cross Code Campaign in 1977 featured a display which included a real life Green Cross Man modelled, it appeared on Superman, and mobile displays, posters and slogans like the one seen here in Heywood. This was the latest in a series of campaigns instigated by the Rochdale Road Safety Committee going back to 1947. The 1949 campaign had an exhibition in the Town Hall and used slogans like 'Keep Death off the Road' and 'A Short Cut May Mean a Long Ride To Hospital' as warnings to drivers. The Green Cross campaign was a national initiative aimed at children using television advertisements, posters and other literature to get its message across. It was generally activity based and schools were encouraged to hold Road Safety Weeks as part of the curriculum. Hill Top Primary School at Kirkholt was a typical example of what school activities took place. Rochdale Police loaned some traffic lights which were placed at the entrance to the school so at playtime and lunchtime the children had to obey the lights before they entered and left the building. A teacher, Jennifer Bridges, wrote a song for the children to sing. Graphs were made showing how many teachers wore seat belts and, as the school backed on to the M62, the children were able to carry out 'seat belt spottings' and present their findings as part of their project.

A car enthusiast's delight as we look across from the Town Hall towards the bottom of Yorkshire Street. It is almost like looking at the history of the British motor car if you look at the Fords, the Minis, the Vauxhalls, the Humbers and more besides and then wonder what did happen to the British car industry. Driving and parking seems to be quite a relaxed affair and to be a pedestrian and cross to the Post Office without the aid of a zebra crossing looks as easy. It is hard to believe that these cars and buses are standing on a bridge which covers the River Roch and at 445 metres is the widest bridge in Europe. Built over a period of 23 years and completed in 1926 it was and still is a major feat of engineering and without it this part of town, especially the Esplanade which enhances the Town Hall, would not look as grand nor would the relative ease of traffic, pedestrian and motor, be as evident. The buildings in view, like Barclays and Midland Banks, adopt a grand status of their own as they appear to guard the entrance to Yorkshire Street. To their left is the old William Deacons Bank now the Royal Bank of Scotland, before it acquired its colonnade, and further to the left is the ABC cinema with Hardman's Mill and the tower of St. James's Church at the rear.

What a parade!

The banner of St James Church Sunday School is held high in the 1964 Whit Walk. This traditional public affirmation of faith had one innovation this year in that it was the first time that the 4000 Anglicans and Non-Conformists walked together. Behind them were the Roman Catholics and then the Ukrainian Churches' representatives. At this time the ecumenical spark was beginning to flicker and to a great majority of churchgoers that public demonstration would be seen as a welcome symbol in the long process of reconciliation.

The walks of the 1960s were regarded as a high point in the proud tradition. The vast majority of the local churches were represented by Sunday School children, Rose Queens, Scouts and Guides. Each group was headed by a banner and some by a symbol of faith like a white Bible in front of the Band of Hope contingent or an icon borne by the Ukrainian boys or a lamb at the head of the St Patrick's Church procession. Bands like the one from the Church for the Destitute or from village Prize bands played as the procession made its way to the gardens below the Parish Church.

The 'Rochdale Observer's' comment that while young people in the south of England were boiling over into gang warfare on Whit Sunday, thousands in Rochdale were not afraid to continue to observe the tradition of making their Christian witness in public' seems an appropriate one to have been made.

Left: All the hard work in preparing to put on a pantomime seems to have paid off for members of the Rochdale Catholic Theatre Guild as they pose happily for the camera ready to give their all in the production of 'Aladdin' in January 1964 at St John's Church.There is something for everyone in the show, dancing, singing, slapstick comedy and subtle humour and even an impersonation of those four rapidly rising stars from Liverpool. The dancers have been well trained by Beryl Brinkman and the highly nervous producer is Alf Worrall. There is something deeply satisfying to be part of a group of people who work together to put on a show like this whether you are the lead like Doreen Byrne as Aladdin or Vincent McNicholas as the Emperor or Maureen Sumner and Nicholas Byrne as Pekoe and Abanazer respectively. Or whether you had a minor part like Sharon Denvir, Ian Garside, Lynn Dear and John Vale or you got all the laughs like Billy Shearin as Widow Tankey and like Peter Dawson and Eric Walton as Tu Hi and Tu Lo. Or you had the grand sounding part of Vizier and had to work hard to perfect your Liverpool and Chinese accents or you were Una Kelly who was Sophie. The audiences certainly enjoyed the show especially when Tu Hi mysteriously turned To Lo into Mrs Twankey and there was a full house almost every night.

Above: The tradition of performing the Pace Egg Play at Eastertime had been carried on for many years in the old Rochdale cattle market performed by travelling players who by and large stuck to a basic plot rather like today's pantomimes. There was always the hero, a fool and the evil doer who in the end gets his just desserts, usually after a 'bloody' fight. The insults between the players never changed and usually revolved round diseases you could get or be inflicted with. The trouble was that later often the plot was forgotten and the fight started earlier and earlier or the players forgot tradition and treated it as a money-making venture. So two old boys of the Rochdale Secondary School took it upon themselves in 1928 to present the 'authentic' more genteel version. The script was rewritten using the original Rochdale script and others from different parts of the country. The play was entitled, 'Play of St George of the Knights and the Dragon ' with all the parts taken by pupils, the main ones being St.George, the Black Prince, the Doctor and Dirty Bet. The play then became a tradition with the honour always falling to boys of Clement Royds House to perform it in the Great Hall. Despite not taking part Sir Cyril Smith always enjoyed the play especially as the school was allowed home earlier afterwards.

The preparations for Whitworth's May 1964 Carnival, the first for three years, took place in the hottest weather of the year yet, when Saturday dawned, thunderstorms were on the 'weather menu'. Rain did hold off for the rickety old car equipped with battered old luggage with the four hillbillies just as bedraggled as in the television show (above). They came to a sudden stop when the vehicle overheated but, after emergency treatment involving a bucket of water, the car sped off at a steady 5mph. Other entries noted for their humour were from A. Normanton & Sons' 'Hawaiian Eye' and Cassius Clay versus Sonny Liston both of whom appeared to be regulars in the Whitworth Arms.

Judith Varley on her horse Bisquit (left) as St. George and the Dragon was the winner of the Best Horse Mounted Competition. A sign of the changing times - the expected trouble between local Mods and Rockers from Rawtenstall proved to be nothing more than a rumour, although the police took it seriously enough to have extra men on stand-by. Another sign of things to come - the organisers were worried about vandals damaging the cricket field. That did give the local scouts the chance to camp out there on the Friday night and nothing untoward occurred much to everyone's relief, including, no doubt, the scouts. The last event of the carnival was the one to suffer from the weather when, just as Whitworth and Healey Prize Band was set to play, the heavens opened. Otherwise the day had been a great success in one respect in that the amount of money that was raised was the same as in 1961 and it helped to expand the Meals on Wheels Service and to increase the number of Christmas parcels sent to the local old folk.

At Whitworth's May 1964 Carnival, a more serious note was struck by the children of Hallford Congregational Church with their 'Suffer Little Children' (main picture) and those from St John's, Facit with their version of The Good Samaritan. Millgate Baptist Church children's entry 'Sing a Song of Sixpence'(inset) was the joint winner of the procession floats along with Shawforth Methodist Church's 'Achievements 1953-63'. Like all carnivals and locally organised events then, it did reflect a community spirit, one which is not so prevalent now on such a large scale as this as people have developed other interests and other ways of using their leisure time but there is still a surge of feeling today when fund raising for a good cause is undertaken.

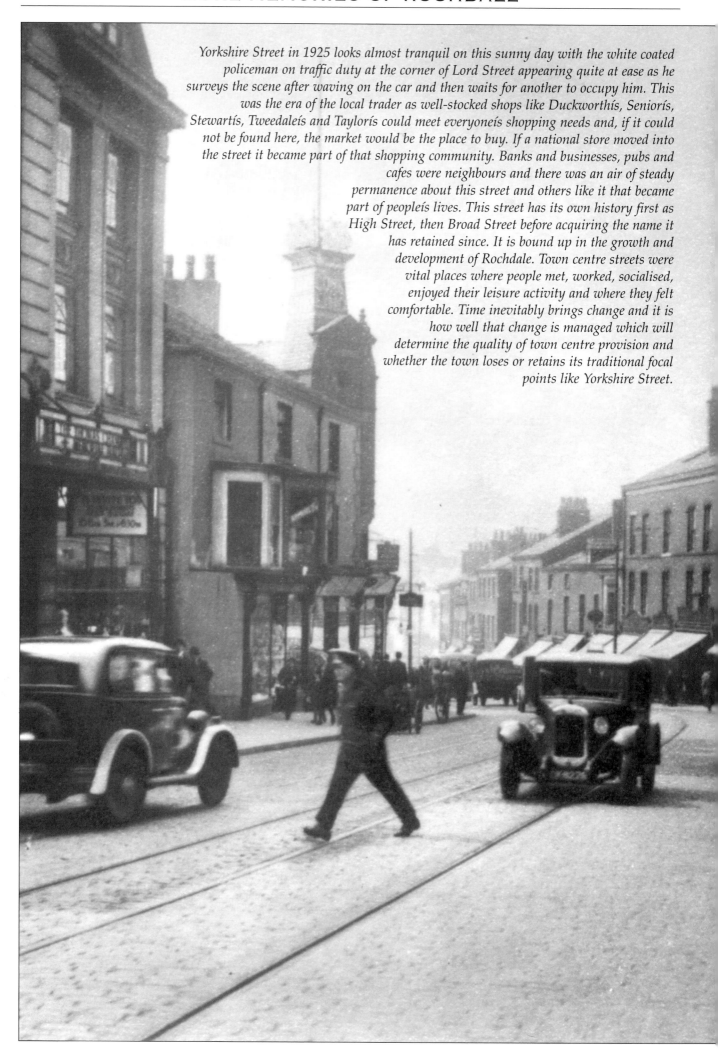

Yorkshire Street in 1925 looks almost tranquil on this sunny day with the white coated policeman on traffic duty at the corner of Lord Street appearing quite at ease as he surveys the scene after waving on the car and then waits for another to occupy him. This was the era of the local trader as well-stocked shops like Duckworth's, Senior's, Stewart's, Tweedale's and Taylor's could meet everyone's shopping needs and, if it could not be found here, the market would be the place to buy. If a national store moved into the street it became part of that shopping community. Banks and businesses, pubs and cafes were neighbours and there was an air of steady permanence about this street and others like it that became part of people's lives. This street has its own history first as High Street, then Broad Street before acquiring the name it has retained since. It is bound up in the growth and development of Rochdale. Town centre streets were vital places where people met, worked, socialised, enjoyed their leisure activity and where they felt comfortable. Time inevitably brings change and it is how well that change is managed which will determine the quality of town centre provision and whether the town loses or retains its traditional focal points like Yorkshire Street.

Shopping spree

Below: This is an early 1930s view of Drake Street from its junction with Water Street. It is at this time Rochdale's other main shopping area and we can see some of the traditional buildings and businesses that made it such a busy street. Timpson's shoe shop stands next to the grand Champness Hall and further down the left hand side is Ivesons' high quality furniture store. Cross over the road and there is another furniture store, Orrell's, and then W. T. Carter, the photographer, and on to Fashion Corner. This road into town from the south also led to the railway station and with that traffic and the amount of shops it was a very busy thoroughfare, bustling with shoppers. Now, unfortunately, it is a shadow of its former self. Iveson's and Fashion Corner are closed and so are many other of the shops that made the street so popular only Butterworths, the jewellers, remaining. The traffic is still busy these days but the street appears to have lost that vitality it must have had before the commercial centre of gravity of the town moved into shopping centres and supermarkets. The major buildings of note remaining are Champness Hall still functioning and the offices of the 'Rochdale Observer'. Everything appears forlorn and the empty shop that was Iveson's is a symbol of what Drake Street used to be like and what has been allowed to happen to it.

Above: The bottom of Yorkshire Street looking up the hill towards Seniors Outfitters and the Market with Duckworth's the Grocers on the right. Above the shop is a coal, coke and, a sign of the times, smokeless fuel merchants. Outside Duckworth's at the corner of The Walk is a gas lamp situated over a ventilator for the main sewer with the flame of the lamp constantly lit to sterilise the flames. The basic plan of the street has not changed over the years when it was old pack-horse route to Halifax. The market buildings stretch from the junction with Lord Street left to Toad Lane and back across to Yorkshire Street. This was the premier shopping street of the town full of established local businesses, Then national chains moved in and shops like Duckworth's closed. People's shopping habits and lifestyles changed and town planners needed to plan. Streets like this one had to change as there came out of town supermarkets and town centre shopping malls which paid very little attention to the architecture of the buildings they either replaced or were situated beside. As a result there came a hotchpotch of the old with the often shapeless new and it is only now that planners are looking critically at what has happened to town centres as they try to breathe new life into them.

Right: It is what you can just see in this photograph of Lord Street before it was swallowed up in the area's re-development that is of interest for it is the re-building of the outside market at the rear of the shop that creates this interest. There had always been an outdoor market in the town and a market had stood at the bottom of Yorkshire Street since the sixteenth century. By the 1960s there was the Upper Market Hall, the New Market and the original Lower Market. Long time market shoppers in Rochdale have seen many changes either as a result of fire which severely damaged the Open Vegetable Market at the junction of Toad Lane and Lord Street in 1937 or redevelopment when the town's Market Hall was demolished in 1975 to make way for a new shopping centre incorporating another Market Hall. Whether the atmosphere unique to market shopping still remains in the new surrounds is of course a personal matter. However, there does not appear to be the noise and bustle associated with the old style 'free-standing' markets but in an age where value for money is important then perhaps shoppers can manage without those things. What did happen in the demolition of this area was to change the face of this part of the town without possibly retaining the character of shops like B&M and of pubs like The Old Clock Face which stood on the corner of Toad Lane and Lord Street.

"IN THE 1960s, COBBLE-STONES WERE STILL IN EVIDENCE"

Parking restrictions were neither absent or ignored on this stretch of Yorkshire Street in the late 1960s. There were still cobblestones, along the street and the Market Hall was not yet rebuilt after the 1937 fire. It was a chilly day when the picture was taken - a clue being the number of turned-up collars, hands in pockets and warm headgear visible on the many passers-by.

The Neville Reed sign is the most obvious bit of advertising along the street but keen eyes will be able to make out Seniors' shop on the prominent corner position higher up the street. Seniors was established in 1919 by Sidney Senior.

At work

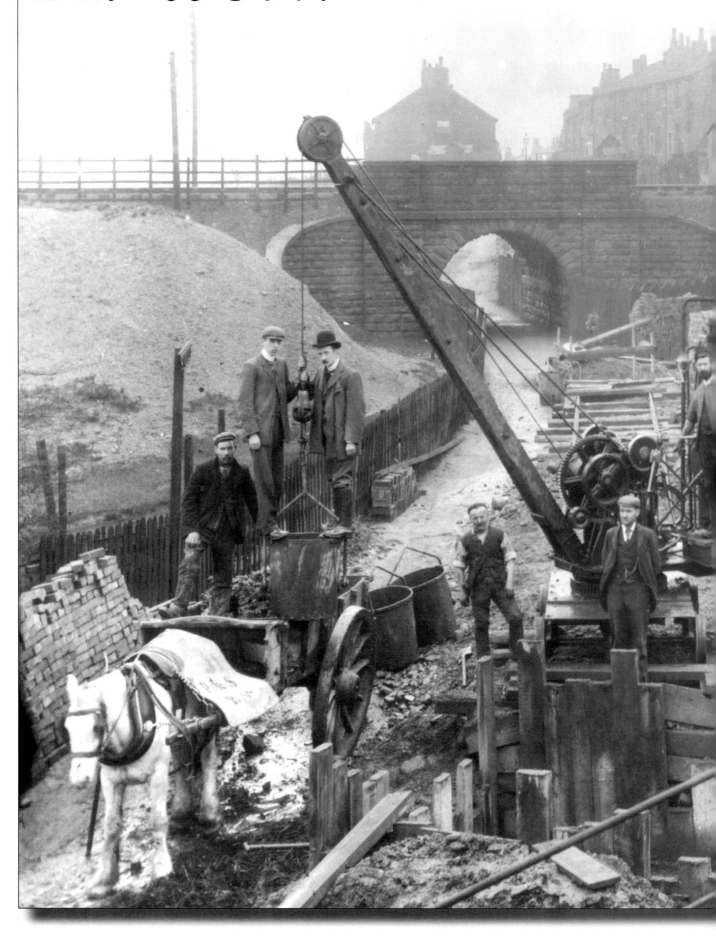

The massive growth in the population of Rochdale in the latter part of the nineteenth century was due to the spread of industry in the area mainly as a result of the increased demand for cotton and associated products. Factories expanded and more and more houses were built. The people of the town had to live, eat and sleep and so the public's health became a matter of urgent concern not only in terms of the need for medical facilities, hospitals and doctors but also for the people themselves to have the opportunity to live healthier lives. Towns like Rochdale realised they had a public responsibility to look after their citizens and provide for them services which we take for granted today. Public Health then became a priority as the risk of disease from sewerage and waste products was everywhere, in factories, shops, schools and houses, Here we see council workmen laying sewerage pipes in the town as part of the operation to construct an intercepting sewer for the Stanney Brook Valley along Belfield Lane and Newbold Street. This would be a slow and laborious and, just by looking at this 1899 photograph, an often dangerous task. Engineers will examine with great interest the machinery in use here and the methods of work employed, No hard hat area here!

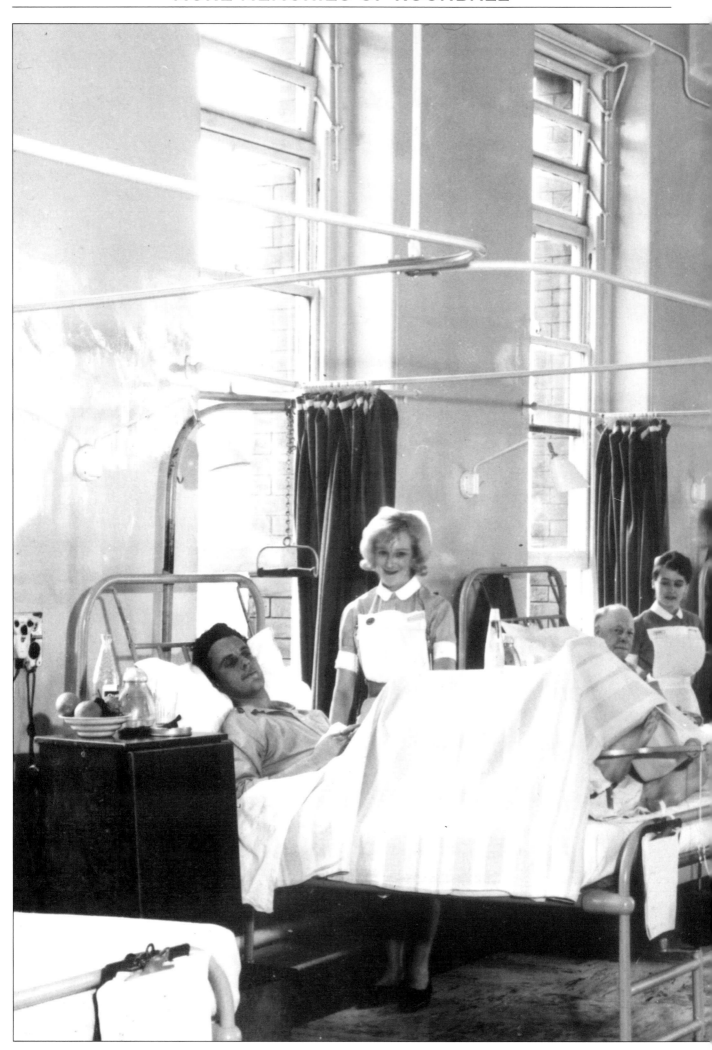

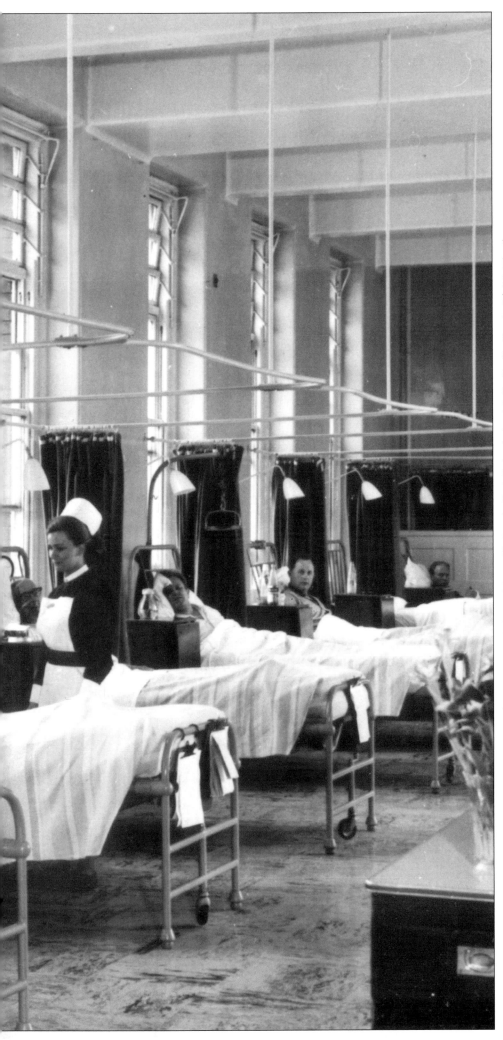

Whether you are supposed to look so contented being in the Rochdale Infirmary is doubtful but when you consider how well you appear to be looked after then, perhaps, a smile of satisfaction is in order here. The story of the growth of hospital services in Rochdale would be little different to any other town. Accommodation for the sick was always as great a need as preventing sickness as the Infirmary struggled to provide suitable accommodation and treatment, especially before the advent of the National Health Service and free treatment in 1948. Before the war schemes like the Rochdale Infirmary Contributory Scheme of four old pence per week paid for you and your family's treatment, As services have been extended and equipment become more sophisticated, staff have had to be more highly trained and the Infirmary has had to adapt to meet those needs. Fortunately many of the diseases which were almost untreatable in the past can now be prevented or quickly dealt with. One example is the way that anyone with scarlet fever was once treated. Memories of fever ambulances, red blankets, no visitors, a coal-fired ward in the local Isolation Hospital, weeks of convales-cence, milk puddings, barley in stews and 'stoving' your belongings to sterilise them. Times really have changed for the better.

Left: This photograph taken in 1940 is of the Auxiliary Fire Service unit at Norden before the arrival of a self-propelled pump when their equipment was just a towing vehicle and trailer pump. The men of this unit look quite confident and competent here and may well have been but that would not be the case in many other towns and cities of the country, where the accommodation offered to the men in one city achieved special notoriety. The A.F.S. was born out of necessity in response to heavy German bombing of Britain's industrial conurbations when it was obvious that the Regular Fire Service could not cope. However there was a drastic shortage of equipment and in London taxicabs were requisitioned and painted grey or green and did the work of fire-appliances. Many men in the A.F.S. were part-time and did a day's work before reporting for duty where they served one night on duty, one night on call and one, if they were lucky, free. Training was rare and often they were not held in high regard by their regular colleagues or by members of the public. These men worked long hours in dangerous conditions, having been given the 'dirty' jobs like pumping out flooded cellars or air-raid shelters. It is no wonder that many were injured or even killed or suffered because of illness or stress. From the demeanour of these men at Norden it seems they did not undergo the traumas of their colleagues in larger towns and cities.

Above: Police dog, Kim, with his handler P.C. Jim Ogden aided and abetted by P.C. 'Sailor' Gooderham is being put through his paces as part of the 1955 inspection of police. The Chief Constable of Rochdale, Major J.S. Harvey had just persuaded the Borough Police Authority that the exceptional olfactory powers of dogs could be utilised effectively in association with police work.

These measures were part of a package of innovations and developments which were deemed necessary as the amount and incidence of crime increased and the duties of police were widened accordingly. Alsatians and Labradors were considered to be best suited to this kind of work and approval had been given to introduce a section of three dogs. Both handlers and dogs were trained at the Metropolitan Police Training Centre.

The dogs and their handlers were responsible for nine arrests in 1955 with Major Harvey reporting that 'Criminals and hooligans have shown a strong disinclination to stay and argue when police dogs are about'. This is hardly surprising! The teams were well-known in the town and thrilled the crowds at local shows when the dogs were put through their paces in displaying their tracking and attacking skills with the chief concern always being for the poor volunteer who was being tracked and attacked.

The beginning of the end as the land to the left of Toad Lane around Lord Street and Blackwater Street is cleared to make way for the new shopping precinct. Ready to go are the many long established shops and businesses which were at the heart of this part of town in streets such as Brickcroft and Temple Street. What remained, as we can see, are the Pioneers (formerly the Provident) Co-operative Stores. Behind was the Red Lion Hotel which like the Old Clock Face suffered under the developer's hammer. To the right is the covered market area which would be incorporated into the new centre thus reducing Toad Lane to a mere lane rather than a major thoroughfare. Two churches catch the eye. At the top of Toad Lane stands St Mary's, Wardleworth which survived and still flourishes despite being tagged on to the dual carriageway. The other is St James Church whose tower can be picked out as it stands at the western end of town. Unfortunately it is no longer a centre of worship and stands almost forlornly in the middle of a roundabout. To its left as though standing on tip-toe wanting to be seen are the two chimneys and top floors of Townhead Mills. Whether the arrival of shopping centres and the demise of small businesses were a good thing for towns like Rochdale is a matter for debate but what did happen was to change the face of the town and this development was only the start.

The changing face of waste water treatment

Biwater Treatment Ltd is the result of an amalgamation of three companies, Ames Crosta Ltd, Whitehead & Poole and William Farrar Ltd, each having a long history in sewage and the water industry.

Ames Crosta developed from general jobbing engineers, James Mills & Company. They became aware of the large potential market in the municipal water industry and in 1900 the Ames Crosta Sanitary Engineering Company became sales agents for the Mills' products.

A local sewage works manager, Joshua Bolton, moved to Bury where he helped to develop an activated sludge treatment process which became known as the Simplex aeration plant. James Mills built his experimental machinery and later Bolton agreed to Mills and Ames Crosta becoming sole manufacturers of his invention. His son, Frank Bolton became a director of James Mills in 1923.

In 1926 the company was reconstituted as Ames Crosta Mills, known for the next 50 years as ACM. Activities concentrated at Heywood from where over 250 Simplex aeration plants were installed throughout the world. Soon ACM was installing

complete projects in sewage and trade effluent treatment. The quality was such that some are still in service in different parts of the world today.

During the Second World War production capacity was diverted into other channels. After the war new sewerage schemes were demanded and the company's facilities had to expand to meet the demand.

In 1960 ACM became part of the Woodall Duckham Group. This led to a new phase of growth. By the mid sixties the company had introduced the Archimedean screwpump to the UK market. Soon afterwards the company acquired United Filters and Engineering Ltd of Mitcham (UFE) who had been specialists in water treatment for over 70 years and were recognised experts in swimming pool installation and treatment. The two companies worked independently but conferred over each other's pollution problems.

Another takeover changed the company name to Ames Crosta Babcock Ltd. In 1977 the company formally merged with UFE, (now Babcock Water Treatment Ltd) and the water treatment work was moved to Heywood. Then, after over 150 years in the

Left: The fully automated plant operation of Rivington WTW.
Above: "The offices" at Gregge Street, Heywood.

emergency occurred. There were also oil rig requirements.

Meanwhile, the company's normal activities were expanding again. Water treatment plants were produced for Anglian and Severn Trent Water, the former being particularly prestigious.

Since the firms came together on the Heywood site there has been a steady expansion in the traditional water markets with additional work in areas covered by the new Water Asset Management Division.

Today, Biwater's expertise is widespread, offering water systems investment and management, water and environmental engineering, and water and wastewater products and services. They are unique in being able to offer a complete in-house

town centre, manufacturing work was transferred to a brand new factory on the outskirts of the town. The office staff of the combined companies moved there too in 1977.

In the same year the company won a £72 million contract for a water treatment plant in Saudi Arabia. It was the first where they took responsibility for all aspects of the job including civil engineering. Other large contracts followed, mainly in the Middle East. The company was glad of them as the home market at this time was hit by recession and the re-organisation of its customer base as water authorities were established.

By 1981 the workforce had been reduced to 230 from a peak of 650. This slimmed-down version of the firm soon effected a return to strength. Experimental work was done for the Royal Navy on water desalination. Fresh water facilities were urgently needed when the Falklands

service to their clients with process, civil, mechanical, electrical and chemical engineers and resources at their disposal. Biwater works closely with its clients to achieve the highest quality standards and prides itself on the care with which it approaches both environmental and health and safety issues.

Above: "The works" at Gregge Street, Heywood. Below left: Eastbourne underground marine treatment works under construction. Below right: Eastbourne Marine Treatment works.

Providing a personal insurance service

Mr James Winstanley had been an insurance agent for Co-operative Insurance for some time when, in 1961 he decided to branch out on his own and founded the West Pennine Insurance Group.

The business had small beginnings, being run initially from Mr Winstanley's home in Todmorden Road with a staff of three, Mr Winstanley himself, his wife and part time help from a neighbour. These days the business is run by their daughter Anne and son Peter, whilst Mr Winstanley senior is semi-retired, being on hand to advise.

Other members of the family are involved, including James Winstanley's brother-in-law, David Mather and his son Andrew.

After two years the business was able to move from the Winstanley home to 84, Church Street, Littleborough for a rent of £30 a quarter.

The year 1968 saw the first branch of the business outside Littleborough. This was in Oldham and offices followed in Middleton in 1969, Prestwich in 1970 and Reddish in 1972. These made up the Group which currently consists of 25 branches spread throughout the north west.

By 1980 the company owned both the Church Street building at number 84 and also the premises next door.

In 1975 the administration of the business had moved to Victoria Street, Littleborough. In 1986 the business purchased the Old Post Office which is now the headquarters of the group.

West Pennine is involved in all aspects of the insurance business. Motor insurance forms the largest sector, followed by household insurance and there is a well patronised separate commercial department for fleets of vehicles. Other sectors deal with properties and liabilities.

The company carries a professional indemnity policy of £2 million for the protection of their clients. More recently the company has set up 'Quoteline' to compete with the direct insurance market.

"A CONSIDERABLE NUMBER OF HIS ORIGINAL CUSTOMERS ARE STILL WITH THE COMPANY TODAY"

Offering personal service from a family-run business, the company plans further expansion in the north west and a major investment in computers to take it into the next millennium.

James Winstanley measures his company's track record by the considerable number of his original customers who are still with it today.

Above: The old Post Office at 109 Church Street, Littleborough which is now the company's head office.
Facing page top: Mr James Winstanley, founder of the company, pictured in 1986.
Facing page bottom: The second home to West Pennine Insurance, 84 Church Street, rented initially for £30 a quarter in 1964 and subsequently purchased in 1980.

The little Co-op doing king size business

Unlike most small shops, the little shop in Lanebottom was and is not a family business. The Lanebottom Industrial Equitable Pioneers Society was first registered in 1860, having been founded by local people to take advantage of the Co-operative Movement which had been founded some fifteen years previously in Rochdale.

Its original business activity was retail grocery which was carried on at the same premises the business occupies today, six miles out of Rochdale on an obscure little road in a tiny village.

Lanebottom is the last surviving single small Co-op in Lancashire with its own Board of Management, and where grocery orders were delivered to its customers, at no extra charge, right up until the closure of the grocery side of the business due to lack of sales. Dividends were paid on grocery purchases until December 22nd 1995.

The original shop windows were used for the display of grocery items as well as sundry smaller items. Following the closure of the grocery business the windows have been utilised to display carpets and the shop houses a display of cabinet furniture. Meanwhile the house across the street has been re-modelled by the Co-op staff to display carpets and furniture.

The transformation from a one-shop country co-op was effected in the forties when the then manager had the idea of selling discounted goods to the employees of the CWS in Manchester.

The CWS in the 1970s began the amalgamation of the smaller co-ops into the larger organisations as now seen. The transformation of the Headquarters in and around Manchester and the sales rooms were closed and in most cases demolished to make way for new buildings or altered to office accommodation. Thus with the loss of the "Employee" trade the business became more focused on general retail.

In addition to carpets and furniture, Lanebottom sells electrical appliances, jewellery and watches.

Expansion has continued in the existing locality by new buildings in keeping with their surroundings and by the acquisition of local buildings. The business has established itself in a very competitive field where it is not easy to increase sales year by year. Nevertheless Lanebottom does a quietly flourishing business in the domestic field, selling furniture, floor coverings and domestic electrical goods. Sales are generally to the general public although special agreements are sometimes made, especially with contacts within the co-operative movement.

In 1997 the business with the Co-op and CIS employees and pensioners once again commenced to enable the current employees to have the same privileges as originally offered to the employees when they began working for the organisation.

The main reasons for success are the very reasonable prices of the goods Lanebottom offers which represent far more of a bargain than those offered by multiple furniture stores.

The other big attraction is the personal service customers receive. Whatever their requirements Lanebottom always has the relevant member of staff available with the knowledge that answers every client's queries.

As a past employee has remarked, in spite of the old-fashioned appearance of the original premises with its plank door and tiny windows, 'We're not a museum, we're a working piece.'

Above and below: Two aspects of Lanebottom Industrial Equitable Pioneers Society as it appears today.
Facing page: The premises as they appeared in the 1940s.

Providing a high quality legal service

Documents found in the office cellar in March 1978 by Mr Wright, the then senior partner, have allowed Hartley, Thomas & Wright to trace back their history to 1745.

The local Trade Directories show a Mr Hartley in practice in Rochdale in the later 1800s. He took over an older practice belonging to a Mr Harris.

A number of the members of the Hartley family then continued the practice with various partners and titles until shortly before the Second World War. It was then purchased by Mr Charles Henry Thomas from the then surviving member of the Hartley family. Mr Albert Wright was already employed by the firm, initially as an office junior but later becoming an articled clerk.

The war interrupted both the running of the practice and Mr Wright's articles. Mr Wright served in the Royal Navy whilst Mr Thomas was called up to do Army service in time for the D Day Landings.

When peace was declared, both returned to the practice and Mr Wright qualified and became a partner. Since that time the firm has been known as Hartley, Thomas & Wright. The practice was later joined by Peter Battle who later became a partner and Mr Kendal Lindley who, when he qualified, joined the partnership and managed the firm's Todmorden office, practising there from the early 70s in his own name.

Changes in the next nine years included Mr C H Thomas' retirement, Mr Battle's retirement due to

ill-health and from 1978 to 1981 a move for the firm into temporary accommodation in the Prudential Buildings on South Parade and premises in Drake Street whilst the Nat-West Bank in Town Hall Square was refurbished.

Mr Wright carried on as sole practitioner until 1979 when Mr Peter Riley joined the firm as an assistant solicitor. He became a partner in 1980.

Back in Town Hall Chambers, the Practice took in Mr Roger Addington as an assistant solicitor in 1982. Later in the same year Mr Wright retired, leaving Mr Riley as sole practitioner. In 1983, Mr Addington was taken into partnership whilst Mr Thomas and Mr Wright remained as consultants to the firm.

Since that date the firm has continually expanded. In early 1990 an additional office was opened in Yorkshire Street where the Conveyancing and

Probate Departments were based. In 1995 partnership was offered to Miss Sally Clark who had been associated with the firm since 1991 and Mr John Binks who had been articled with the firm in the eighties and rejoined it in 1991.

Throughout its long history the practice has been general. However, the present partners believe in the need for increasing specialisation and diversification of activities. They have therefore developed the firm from a predominantly conveyancing and probate practice to providing a full range of legal services and expertise.

A Property Sales Service has been introduced at a competitive rate and with the added benefit of the firm's complete control over the progress of the sale of Clients' properties.

Thus the firm provides a high quality service to all its clients who pay it back by returning and recommending to others.

Left: *Packer Steet, Rochdale pictured in 1866, with Mr Harris's practice on the top floor of the building later to become Town Hall Chambers.*
Below: *The current partners pictured from left to right; Roger G. Addington, John S. Binks, Sally A. Clarke and Peter A. Riley outside Town Hall Chambers.*

Carving out a niche in the building trade

Until the mid forties, Messrs Walter Leach and Arthur Clegg worked as joiners for a local firm, James Fielden, Joiners. In 1946 they decided to purchase the business.

Taking premises at Meadowhead Saw Mills, Milnrow, they became partners in a business that offered services in joinery, building and undertaking.

They stayed at their first premises for forty years, building up their trade, dropping off the business in building and coffin making to specialise in joinery for the building trade. The hardwood and softwood they began with is still the raw material they use today. The machinery however has changed with the times and they now use modern CNC equipment.

Three generations of Cleggs have now served in the business, including Peter and Jonathon.

In 1987 the business moved a short distance to improved premises, also in Milnrow, at Lily Street Mills. Here they turn out new and replacement windows, bespoke doors, staircases and other joinery products for builders, double glazing companies and other joinery companies. Being able to manufacture specialist products, such as ready-hung doors and special staircases, made with up to the minute machinery and tooling, Leach and Clegg occupy a secure and welcome place in Rochdale's trade and industry.

Above: From left to right Peter, Arthur and Jonathon Clegg. Below: Staff of Leach and Clegg Joinery Manufacturers.

Improving the profile of Rochdale

The Wheatsheaf Shopping Centre was built by Chesterfield Properties in 1990.

The Centre takes its name from the original Wheatsheaf Public House and incorporates the pub's original arch. The keystone is the source of the logo of the original Rochdale Pioneers.

Soon after it opened the centre won an architectural award, its main feature being the stained glass window depicting the chimneys and bales of wool to emphasise the history of the wool industry in Rochdale.

The management proudly believes that the centre improves the profile of Rochdale town centre, especially since its mini refurbishment in 1996. Six stores were amalgamated, together with one mall area and one cafe to form a massive single store for T J Hughes. The management and staff are very active in all Town Centre activities and

the Centre is very user friendly, especially for disabled shoppers and families with prams.

Surrounded by Yorkshire Street, Penn Street and Baillie Street, the centre has a catchment of 440,000 within a 10km radius. There are parking spaces provided for 750 cars with direct access from the bus station for shoppers using public transport. The many retail tenants waiting to serve them include BHS with its 30,000 square feet department store and T J Hughes whose premises are even larger. The central Library occupies 30,000 square feet and there is a new mall cafe.

The entrance porch is cheerful with its distinctive directories in bright blue with red and white lettering directing shoppers to the many shops within. The atmosphere inside is made pleasant with an abundance of greenery, strategically planted, clever use of natural light and a black and white mosaic floor.

It is not surprising that the centre is a great draw, with its blend of retail entertainment with echoes of the past and its modern facilities.

Top: The impressive entrance into the Wheatsheaf Centre. Above: The welcoming Mall Café area. Left: Another approach into the Wheatsheaf Centre past the central Library.

'The fine art of frying fish' - One hundred years of service

The managing director of V.A. Whitley, Mr Tony Rogers, believes that "Frying good fish and chips is an art form. It has been the purpose of his company since its beginning to supply the various fish frying 'artists' in the north west with the raw materials they need to be creative."

At the turn of the century in North Manchester, 18 years old Vincent Affleck Whitley made the daunting decision to set up in business on his own. With a borrowed £100 he bought a horse and float and opened premises on Russell Road, Blackley. There he supplied oils and fats to the fish frying trade in and around North Manchester.

He soon became a '3 horse-power' business with Kitty, Dorrie and Flo delivering oak casks of South American neatsfoot, groundnut, cottonseed and soya bean oils on a horse drawn wagon. Together with American lard, beef dripping and 'compound' in wooden crates they comprised the basic frying essentials of the age.

The wagon also carried the other staple commodities the trade needed; sacks of marrowfat peas, batter-flour, salt, soda and vinegar. From the beginning, 'Vin' provided quality goods and an excellent service.

Immediately after the First World War, V.A. Whitley & Co bought a second hand Ford model-T van replaced in the twenties with an 'A series'. The Ford model B added in 1932 remained the backbone of the fleet till 1954. There are company legends about 'the old BB'. In 1924 the company started producing its own high quality batters.

In 1936 Vin's son in law Mil Rogers joined the company. The difficult trading years after the Second World War left it still in business but in very poor shape. Vin's death in 1950 was a severe blow but Mil Rogers struggled through the fifties to develop the company.

By the early sixties with business on the upturn, larger premises were needed. Facilities in Hill Lane, Blackley were bought though the offices remained in a house in Russell Road. Mr Rogers needed help and his son Tony left the teaching profession for the trade of fish frying that he had grown up with.

Lack of capital meant that expansion had to be gradual and vehicles second-hand, though reliable. Tony believed in 'backing Britain' and

Above: Vincent Affleck Whitley founder of the firm. **Right:** *An early delivery truck outside the original stables in Russell Road.*

Midlands. The offices at Heywood have been refurbished and extensions are being added to the main building.

Today Whitleys offer customers a 'one stop' supply of quality products at competitive prices. In fact, the fourth generation of management emulates the first.

persuaded his colleagues to go "solid Leyland" and the company has retained a BL fleet ever since, providing a high standard of distribution to the fish frying and catering trades.

In 1975, after a three year search for an all-British flagship for the fleet, a vintage 14/28 Flatnose Morris Cowley van was discovered in Great Yarmouth. The company undertook the restoration in its own workshop using a postcard from 1899 to check the signwriting.

Manchester Corporation's redevelopment programme in Blackley reluctantly forced V.A. Whitley to move their premises to Fir Street, Heywood in 1974. At least their proximity to the motorway network ensured fast and efficient distribution throughout the north-west.

Recently the company has expanded its business into supplying a wide range of frozen goods. The list contains several varieties of frozen-at-sea fish, as well as sausages, burgers, chicken products, pies and pizza products.

Whitleys has three depots, two in Blackpool and north Wales, and the main depot and head office in Heywood, all of which hold the Seafish Wholesaler Quality Award. Orders are now delivered in a 22-van fleet covering the Lake District to mid Wales and across to the West

Top left: *The faithfully restored 14/28 Flatnose Morris Cowley van making a delivery on Whitworth Road, Rochdale.* *Top right*: *An aerial view of the Heywood premises. Above: Deliveries being made 'One hundred years on'!* *Below*: *The current directors of the firm, from left to right, Chris Rogers, Tony Rogers (Managing Director) and Brian Scott.*

A centre for engineering excellence

In the mid 1960s the engineering manufacturers of Rochdale and the then newly formed Engineering Industry Training Board set about to improve the training of apprentices for their industry. There were two groups formed, namely Rochdale Engineering Group Training School and the Roch Group Training School.

These groups were merged in the early eighties taking the new name of Rochdale Training Association and setting up in their present Fishwick Street premises.

The company is registered as a charity and is limited by guarantee. It has a board of directors selected from companies within the area. It is committed to providing high quality training and to offering companies and individuals a wide variety of training requirements and advice.

Facilities include fully equipped practical workshops, on-site project work and conference facilities, together with a professional team of experienced staff.

The Association's work has been influenced by changes in Government Training policies and funding methods. Since 1982 it has worked as a major provider for Youth Training Schemes and in 1988 became involved in Adult Training Schemes and specialises now in Engineering, Information Technology, Administration, Customer Care and Prevocational Language Courses.

A range of commercial short courses, tailored to suit the needs of local companies, are also on offer.

In 1997 the Association received a three-year grant from the European Social Fund, in conjunction with Rochdale Training Enterprise Council. This has enhanced facilities at the Centre turning it into a Centre of Engineering Excellence.

Left: Students proudly display the results of their Microlight aircraft project. **Top right:** Students on the Information Technology Courses.

Where the customer comes first

The Mabyrn Rubber Company was established in 1970 and was initially run from the home of Mr Stanley Mason.

In those early days the work comprised mainly of repairing the rubber linings in Road Tankers and was carried out at the customers' site, but as the company became established it became necessary to find a permanent home. Eventually premises were obtained at the present address in Dyehouse Lane, Smallbridge, Rochdale.

Mabyrn's customer list has grown considerably over nearly thirty years but it still includes those very first customer paying testament to the standard of work and personal service provided by Mr Mason and his company.

Mabyrn are specialists in the inspection, application and repair of all types of chemical plant linings. They are also able to provide a fabrication service for pipework and tank fittings of which

they always carry a comprehensive stock. Facilities at the Britannia Works allow for the handling of large chemical plant. With its specialist knowledge of rubber linings for bulk liquid carriers, Mabyrn is able to give sounder guarantees, resulting in the most economic service to its customers. These are mainly the chemical industries and bulk liquid hauliers. Whoever they are, large or small, Mr Mason makes the customer requirements his own.

Above: A large brine filter vessel.
Below: An aerial view of Mabyrn Rubber Company in the early days at the Dyehouse Lane Site.

Catering for the discerning palate

The property at 2, Edenfield Road, Rochdale, which is now the After Eight Restaurant was built as a private residence around 1830. Later it was bought by a local GP who used part of the house as his surgery. Later still it became a hotel, and finally, in 1982, a restaurant.

It was not until 1988 that Geoffrey and Anne Taylor, whose first careers had been in lecturing, both in the UK and in Uganda, took over at the After Eight. The Taylors were in a good position to make a

success of the business as they had two willing daughters to help with the hard work, whilst Mrs Taylor senior could give them the benefit of her long experience in the catering business. She still gives a hand when the restaurant is particularly busy.

Whilst keeping up the standard of fare their customers have grown to expect, the Taylors are busy restoring their premises, with fixtures, fittings and decorations as far as possible in the original early 19th century style. The gardens too are being

furnished with plants that were popular with early Victorian gardeners.

The restaurant is well patronised by local individuals and is often the place chosen by local businesses for entertaining visitors and clients. The Taylors have been hosts for a 'twin-town' delegation, a Nobel prizewinner, many American guests and, once, the Keeper of the Crown Jewels.

All food is freshly cooked on the premises and the restaurant is run as a friendly family establishment. Only the best raw materials are used and the management aims to enable most people to afford to sample first class cuisine.

The After Eight is the first and only Rochdale restaurant to appear in the Michelin Guide. It is also listed in the Good Food Guide. In addition it won two Les Routiers awards, the Corps d'Elite and the Casserole Award.

Left: Tramlines being laid in Rochdale in 1904, with number 2 Edenfield Road in the middle distance.
Above: Yet another award from the Accolade for Catering Excellence. Below: The After Eight Restaurant today, beautifully restored to its former Victorian elegance, both within the house and in the garden.

The right setting for academic achievement

Hopwood Hall College was formed in 1990 from a Borough-wide reorganisation based on the establishment of a three tier school system.

However, in some ways it has a long history since the Middleton Campus contains the original Hopwood Hall dating from the 15th century and a Grade 2 listed building. Also the former chapel of the de la Salle College is at present being proposed by English Heritage for the same status. The chapel was designed by Frederick Gibberd and built in 1964. Finally, there are the remains of a Medieval corn mill, of limited architectural interest but much prized by local historians.

The Middleton campus is set in a beautiful 75 acre parkland originally the Hall grounds. The site was developed from the 1950s by the de la Salle brothers as a teacher training college before it was eventually bought by Rochdale MBC in 1989 to form the base of the new tertiary college.

The town centre site, known as the Rochdale Campus, consists of three main buildings and is the amalgamation of the College of Technology, the Adult Education College and the College of Art and Design. Recently considerable refurbishment work has been undertaken providing a new reception area and Student Mall which was completed in August 1996.

The college is one of the largest employers in the Borough, employing over 180 full time teaching staff, 165 support staff and a large number of part time and fractional appointments. The annual enrolment is about 10,000 students of which 2,500 are full time.

The college has strong links with its community. A number of franchise agreements have been established to meet the training needs of local and national bodies and a range of programmes is offered for students over sixteen following national and regional schemes. There are programmes too for both those in employment and the unemployed. The programmes are guided in-house by college staff and externally by Lifetime Careers.

The college works closely with local employers, Rochdale Business Link and Chamber of Commerce, Rochdale TEC and other large agencies in the NW, having a range of programmes to meet their needs. To meet the needs of partner schools, current developments involve the Internet and the use of Information Technology.

Teaching is not confined to the campus. Seven BTEC Childhood Studies students have recently

returned from a Leonardo-funded placement in Bielefeld which included placements in local kindergartens and the design and construction of a Celtic knot herb garden. Thirty students from GNVQ (Adv) IT and HND Business Studies went to the Baldersdale Youth Hostel in County Durham to take part in a three day residential course. Language students from Hopwood Hall took part in a week long exchange with Spanish students.

The college's achievements are reflected in its continuing improvement in examination performance.

Top left: *The chapel, designed by Frederick Gibberd.*
Top right: *The Rochdale town centre campus.* **Above:** *Some of the College's higher education graduates with the college principal and local MP.*
Left: *Staff and student work together, accessing the internet in one of the I.T. training rooms.*
Facing page top: *The listed building of Hopwood Hall.*
Facing page bottom: *One of the teaching blocks on the Middleton Campus.*

Critical components with complete confidence

United Springs Ltd was formed for the sole purpose of supplying precision springs to all branches of engineering including aircraft, diesel engine and automotive industries, there being an obvious need for a precision spring specialist to meet the demands of an increasingly hi-tech world.

However, the company had small beginnings with other aims. It was established in 1821 as Robert Riley, a firm of general engineers to the textile mills. The first premises were situated in Mere Lane. From here five generations of Rileys ran the company, the last being Mr Arthur Riley who died in 1965. In 1955 Rileys was floated as a limited company.

In those days there was little or no specialist equipment and everything was made by hand. Both world wars brought a heavy demand for military components and engines and the company prospered as a result. Now, of course, the company uses a large amount of computerised machinery but springs are still hand-made by skilled tradesmen on small order batches.

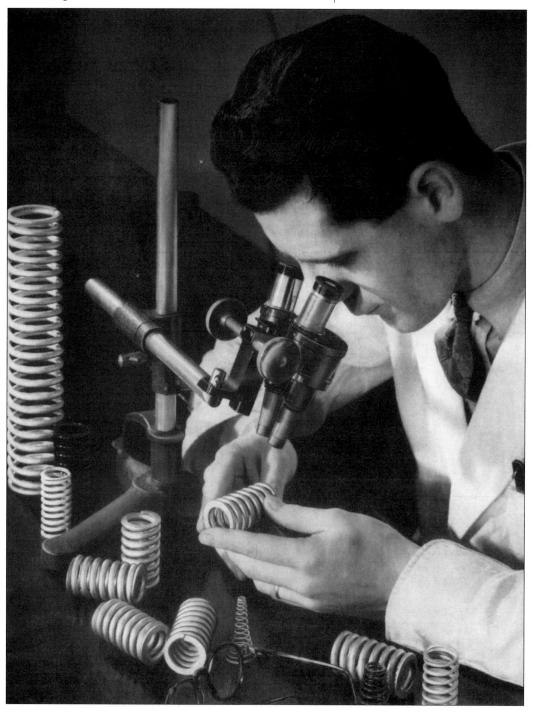

Additional accommodation was purchased in Ambrose Street to meet expanding trade. When saturation point was reached, a new factory was built on Stoneyfield in 1967 and opened by MP Jack McCann. This was purpose built and no doubt enhanced the image of what in those days was little more than a cottage industry.

The 1980s saw a period of considerable change involving mergers, acquisitions and rationalisation affecting a number of established spring manufacturers in the Rochdale area and from which the present day United Springs Limited was born. With this purpose built 65,000 sq. ft. factory on Norman Road together with two

tation of customer requirements through design, material and production control, to on time delivery. Comprehensive in-house facilities including heat treatment, shot peening, plating and metallurgical testing ensuring full control over the manufacturing process.

From tractors to racing cars, buildings to breathing apparatus, the applications for the use of springs is seemingly endless. For this reason United Springs now has the facilities to produce almost any kind of spring - from wire diameters of 0.1mm to springs weighing over 50 kilos.

The Company's links with the past are very tangible - one of its employees - Peter Chisnall started with the firm as an apprentice in 1951 and is still going strong!

With a current £9M turnover (and part of £80M United Industries plc) the Company is well equipped to take on the challenges of the new millennium.

sites in the Midlands it has now become one of the largest spring manufacturing companies in the country - an achievement which the Company believes is in no small part due to the dedication and professionalism of its 150 strong workforce.

Customer satisfaction and technical excellence are critical to the Company's philosophy from interpre-

*Above: Shot Peening to improve the fatigue life of springs. **Below:** United Springs new factory.*
Facing page: *Quality has always been the cornerstone of Robert Riley's success. Photo circa 1950.*

A one-stop shopping trip

Rochdale has been a market town since 1251 when the Royal Charter was granted by King Henry 111. A Market Hall was established in 1824 on a site at the junction of Yorkshire Street and Blackwater Street, where it remained for over 100 years.

In 1872 Rochdale Market Company bought the charter and established a cattle market at the bottom of Manchester Road where the police station presently stands.

In August 1936 Rochdale Corporation bought the Market Charter from the Rochdale Market Company. The old market hall was destroyed by fire in the following year and a temporary home was found for the market in Lea Hall, Smith Street until the new market hall opened in 1939.

It remained on this site until 1975 when the second market hall was demolished to make way for the existing market which was built adjoining the new shopping precinct and was officially opened by HRH Prince Philip. The Shopping Centre itself was opened by Lancashire singing star Gracie Fields in 1978.

The Rochdale Exchange Shopping Centre is the main shopping area within Rochdale, visited by thirteen million people every year. The £8 Million pound refurbishment was begun in 1995 and finished in time for the Christmas trade in 1997.

It transformed the Centre into today's prestigious shopping mall. The work included new lighting throughout, a feature staircase to the balcony cafes, wider aisles for the public to wander around and browse at the open market stalls and the introduction of a baby-changing unit.

Since then the incorporated shops have been refurbished too, together with improvements in the parking arrangements. Facilities are particularly good for the disabled and for families with young children. Now a visit to the centre not only gets the shopping done but also provides a pleasurable experience.

The refurbished Centre is owned by the Co-operative Insurance Society. The Centre manager, Mike Matthews says "We have listened to what the people want and have changed with the times. The constant crowds to be found there suggest that the people of Rochdale agree with him.

Above: Michael Howard with Centre Manager, Mike Matthews.
Left: The impressive exterior of the Exchange.

Leading their field in precision engineering

Venture Precision Engineering Ltd was set up in March 1968. One of its founders, Mr Eddy Lord, still runs the business and Mr Kenneth Hoyle, the other, retired in 1993.

Both men were well prepared for this independent move, having worked for Lewthwaites for years in which they had become thoroughly versed in all aspects of engineering.

To begin with the new business manufactured power pressed tools in premises in the Old East Ward Working Men's Club in Wilfred Street. Today, Ken's son Stephen represents the next generation in the business.

The original premises sufficed until 1978 when a compulsory purchase order meant an enforced move. Venture was by now in a position to build a new factory which was completed in the same year. These premises are still the company base which has been enlarged by the addition of two extra warehouses built in 1981 and a new tool room which was added in 1988.

The main customers for the company's tower packings and valves are in the petro-chemical industry. Venture also produces banding clips and will make most commissioned items from the design stage to completed manufacture. It is one of only two companies in the UK that makes tower packings.

The partners are men of initiative. Once they took a power press and tools to a company in Swaziland to train the

Above: A machine developed and built by Venture for their own use.
Left: The factory production line.

local workers to produce them in their own factories.

The use of tower packings is an old art, the oldest ones having been made from broken stone and coke.

Towards the end of the last century engineers and operators began to appreciate that significant improvements in operation, as well as design, could result from the use of definite shapes, and various plain and modified ring packings were developed. For many years the plain ring was the most universally accepted packing type for equipment for distillation, gas absorption and stripping to the chemical, petroleum and associated industries.

Nowadays there is an extensive range of tower packings made from metals, thermoplastics and ceramic. The first Modern Random Packing good enough to be tested at Fractionation Research Inc. (F.R.I.) was the NUTTER RING™. It remains one of the Worlds leading products in the Mass Transfer Industry . Nutter Engineering are pleased to use the services of Venture Precision

Engineering Co. for the manufacture of their internationally accepted and proven Random Packing. The most advanced design of tower packing currently available is the β-Eta Ring® invented by Mr Ged Horner and Dr Richard Burgess and made in both metal and plastic ranges of materials. All the sizes of the metal β-Eta Ring® are manufactured by Venture Precision Engineering at Rochdale.

Venture Engineering is celebrating its 30th Anniversary and it is the company's proud boast that there has never been an industrial injury to one of its workers. There is currently a new product in the design and patenting stage putting the company in a strong position to enter the next millennium.

Top left: F.R.I. tested Nutter Ring™ Random packing made by Venture.
Above: Various sizes of β-Eta Ring® in a simulated operation - manufactured by Venture exclusively for Eta Process Plant Ltd.
Right: The new logo celebrating the 30th Anniversary.
Below: An aerial view of Venture Precision Engineerings premises taken in 1995.

The town of Rochdale celebrated the Golden Jubilee of its incorporation as a municipal borough in September 1906 in great style.

ACKNOWLEDGMENTS

CLIFFORD C ASHTON

ROCHDALE LOCAL STUDIES LIBRARY

DENNIS PATTISON

H YARWOOD